I0886509

MODELLING BATTLE OF BRITAIN FIGHTER AIRCRAFT

Also by Andy Singleton and in print with Pen & Sword Books:

Painting Wargaming Figures:
WWII in the Desert (2019)

Painting Wargaming Figures:
Early Imperial Romans (2019)

Painting Wargaming Figures:
Rome's Northern Enemies (2020)

Painting Wargaming Figures:
Axis Forces on the Eastern Front (2021)

Painting Wargaming Figures:
Allied Forces in Northwest Europe, 1944–45 (2022)

Painting Wargaming Figures:
Allied Forces in Blitzkrieg Europe, 1939–1940 (2023)

Painting Wargaming Models:
Armoured Vehicles in Europe, 1943–1945 (2024)

MODELLING BATTLE OF BRITAIN FIGHTER AIRCRAFT

ANDY SINGLETON

Pen & Sword
AVIATION

KENT BATTLE OF BRITAIN MUSEUM TRUST

First published in Great Britain in 2025 by
Pen & Sword Aviation
An imprint of
Pen & Sword Books Ltd
Yorkshire – Philadelphia

Copyright © Andy Singleton, 2025

ISBN 978 1 03611 621 7

The right of Andy Singleton to be identified as Author of this work has been asserted by him in accordance with the Copyright, Designs and Patents Act 1988.

A CIP catalogue record for this book is available from the British Library.

All rights reserved. No part of this book may be reproduced, transmitted, downloaded, decompiled or reverse engineered in any form or by any means, electronic or mechanical including photocopying, recording or by any information storage and retrieval system, without permission from the Publisher in writing. NO AI TRAINING: Without in any way limiting the Author's and Publisher's exclusive rights under copyright, any use of this publication to "train" generative artificial intelligence (AI) technologies to generate text is expressly prohibited. The Author and Publisher reserve all rights to license uses of this work for generative AI training and development of machine learning language models.

Typeset in Gill Sans 12/16 by SJmagic DESIGN SERVICES, India.

The Publisher's authorised representative in the EU for product safety is Authorised Rep Compliance Ltd., Ground Floor, 71 Lower Baggot Street, Dublin D02 P593, Ireland.
www.arccompliance.com

For a complete list of Pen & Sword titles please contact

PEN & SWORD BOOKS LIMITED
George House, Units 12 & 13, Beevor Street, Off Pontefract Road, Barnsley, South Yorkshire, S71 1HN, England
E-mail: enquiries@pen-and-sword.co.uk
Website: www.pen-and-sword.co.uk

or
PEN AND SWORD BOOKS
1950 Lawrence Road, Havertown, PA 19083, USA
E-mail: uspen-and-sword@casematepublishers.com
Website: www.penandswordbooks.com

FSC
www.fsc.org
MIX
Paper | Supporting responsible forestry
FSC™ C016779

Contents

Acknowledgements

My sincerest thanks to Dave, Mitch, Scramble and all the volunteers at the Kent Battle of Britain Museum for all their hard work, and Airfix for their very kind and generous support.

I would also like to extend my love and gratitude to my parents and grandparents for taking me to so many air museums, and keeping me supplied with model Messerschmitts, Spitfires and Hurricanes as a child.

Finally, this book is dedicated to all those who served during the Battle of Britain.

Thank you all.

Introduction

The Battle of Britain was the first military campaign to be solely decided by aerial combat. The heavily outnumbered Few of the Royal Air Force defending against masses of German fighters have captured the imagination pretty much since the battle was raging in 1940. Countless books, articles and documentaries have been produced on the subject, arguably few more influential than the 1969 Guy Hamilton movie, which has stirred lifelong interests in Second World War history in so many people, myself included.

The hobby of making model aircraft has existed almost as long as aircraft have existed, and it could even be argued that the hobby pre-dates the Wright Brothers' first flight. Early models were carved from wood and were often built to fly. Kits for collectors started appearing in the early 1930s. The FROG (Flies Right Off the Ground) range of models were supplied as wooden kits of flying aircraft and the Skybirds brand released a range of approximately 1/72 scale wooden kits of a variety of aircraft and airfield buildings.

The first plastic kits were produced by FROG as part of their Penguin range, named after a flightless bird so as not to confuse people with their flying models! These FROG/Penguin models became increasingly popular, and through the war recognition models were used as training aids. These also proved to be popular toys post-war.

In the United Kingdom an Airfix Spitfire Mk I is practically synonymous with the scale-modelling hobby and stems from the aircraft's Battle of Britain legacy. With the first 1/72 Aircraft kit to be released from Airfix being a Spitfire Mk I in 1953, it's easy to understand how it has become so culturally pervasive. Kits have evolved significantly in the past seventy years or so and now feature incredible details and fit, even among the simplest of entry-level models.

(Kent Battle of Britain Museum Collection)

This book stems from childhood visits to the many air museums in the south-east of England, especially to the wonderful Kent Battle of Britain Museum at Hawkinge where one can learn the human stories behind the subjects we enjoy replicating. Most of these museums have an array of model kits available, and these can often be someone's first exposure to the world of modelling. The book is written with the newcomer in mind, but will hopefully also give some inspiration or advice to anyone, no matter how invested they may be into modelling.

1

Workshop

1939 FROG/Penguin Spitfire. This model still has the kit-supplied paint and markings.

GETTING STARTED

Between the world wars, the level of technological advancement was really quite staggering. Aircraft went from canvas-covered biplanes to fast, cannon-armed aluminium monoplanes. Radar entered service, machine guns became lighter and easily portable, and tanks had begun to evolve into incredibly powerful war machines.

In a similar vein, there is a huge and ever-increasing array of hobby products on the market. This array of products is quite overwhelming, even if you have been involved in the hobby for a long time. I'll also attempt to cut through some of the technical terminology, giving a bite-size description of what is required for a few of the most commonly used techniques. Over the last few years there has been the rise of contrast or speed paints by several manufacturers. Now, however, due to space considerations I've not been able to provide guides for these too.

As a solid rule of thumb, when it comes to buying tools you're better off buying better quality. This may prove more expensive, but will work out cheaper in the long run and the results will be more than worth it. That said, it's probably also worth scouring the internet and club mates or friends for reviews to see if an item sounds like something you would find useful and fulfils your specific tastes and needs.

Readers of the other books in this series will be familiar with the following chapter. However, as this book is aimed at the beginner I've repeated it here, partly for completeness but also tailoring it a little to the specific subject matter.

WHAT'S IN A KIT?

The Second World War is probably the most widely supported period for models in any and all scales, with thousands of different products available. Generally speaking, the vast majority of kits are produced in plastic, although some may feature photo-etched metal, resin or even 3D printed parts, while the aftermarket can be expanded to include brass undercarriage legs and gun barrels. White metal used to be a common material for the aftermarket, although this has gradually been replaced by resin as the material of choice for detail parts.

The first plastic kits were those of the FROG/Penguin range, a toy and model range manufactured in the UK with the first release late in 1936. These kits were supplied with paints, glue and transfers, and offered a surprisingly complete range of mostly British aircraft types of the pre- and early war period. These kits were all produced in a constant 1/72 scale

(Copyright Hornby Hobbies Ltd 2025)

and were the first to be a recognizable plastic kit. Airfix would bring out their first aircraft kit in 1953, a Supermarine Spitfire Mk I.

The vast majority of kits available today are injection-moulded plastic in a variety of scales. The age of the tooling or the design of the kit can vary considerably. Most models produced since the mid-1990s tend to be well-fitting with recessed panel lines and details. However, older kits can have more moulding imperfections such as flash or sink marks as well as raised panel lines. The website Scalemates is an invaluable tool for the modeller as one can check for a kit there to determine its provenance and browse the instructions to see if it is something you would want to build.

The complexity of kits has gradually increased over the decades, with their parts counts increasing exponentially. While this can be daunting, working through the model in a logical sequence will see you through.

It's also perfectly reasonable to build kits with simpler engineering. What's important is that you build kits you enjoy and not just what you feel is fashionable as the latter is one way to become quickly bored by the hobby.

Some kits may include etched metal or 3D printed parts. Essentially, cleaning these up is largely the same as working with plastic parts, although with etch it's recommended to cut them from the backing frame using a sharp knife and cutting onto a hard surface such as a kitchen tile to prevent damage to or bending of the part. Either of these materials can then be bonded to the plastic using a superglue-type adhesive.

KNIVES, CUTTERS AND FILES

The first thing you'll need to do, unsurprisingly, is to get the component parts of your model ready for assembly and clean away any residue from the manufacturing process. This can take several forms, but the most common are flash and mould lines which form when the model is being cast in its mould. These appear as either prominent lines around a part, or as chunks or 'worms' of excess material, most especially on edges and undercuts of the component.

These casting imperfections can appear in any material and removing them will massively improve the appearance of the finished model, especially as even a very minor bit of flash or mould line can cause significant fit issues if not fully removed.

HOBBY KNIFE

These broadly fall into two types: those with replaceable blades such as the ubiquitous X-Acto hobby knife and the Stanley knife. Either one of these will probably be your most frequently used tool in preparing your models as the sharp side of the blade can be used for cutting things, while the blunt edge can be used to remove mould lines simply by scraping it down them a few times. This works as the blunt edge is more forgiving of slips and follows the contours of the details well.

Which type of knife you get is entirely up to you, but I'd recommend one of each, especially as they can be found pretty much anywhere that sells tools or hobby supplies for good prices. The replaceable blades of the X-Acto style allow different styles and shapes of blade to be fitted, as well as allowing you to simply replace the blade once it becomes dull.

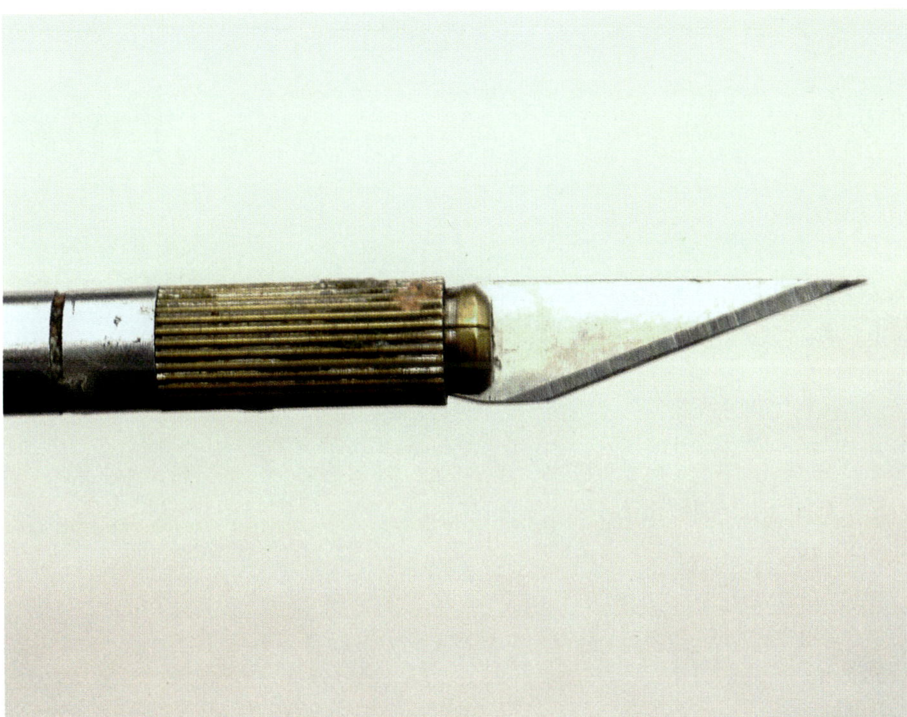

The slender, sharp blades do have their limits, however, as they can blunt quickly when working with metal and may struggle with cutting through thicker plastic sprues as well. They are very sharp though and give you a lot of control, especially for scraping off moulding lines or the remains of tabs after using side cutters. The Stanley knife is handy if you need to do some heavier-duty cutting such as trimming off parts for a conversion that side cutters can't perform as cleanly as you need.

SIDE CUTTERS

Also known as sprue cutters, these are vaguely similar to scissors but with a shorter blade and a more powerful, tensioned action. As the name suggests, these are good at cutting things. Perfect for removing plastic parts from their carrying sprue, it's best to trim the part leaving a small stub of plastic that you can then trim with a knife or file. Also handy for

metal, these can also be used for removing casting lugs or parts from moulding blocks. Sprue cutters can be found in the majority of model shops, both on- and offline.

FILES AND SANDING STICKS

Files can be found in most tool/hardware shops as well as in model and hobby shops. Ideally what you want is a set of jeweller's files or needle files. These typically come in sets of several different files, each being a different shape to allow the cleaning of most parts of a model. A file with a blade more than a centimetre wide will probably prove to be too big for modelling purposes so aim for something quite fine. These are great tools for removing mould lines and getting rid of the contact points of sprue gates.

The more modern sanding solution, however, is sanding sticks or nail-polishing files. These range in gradients of coarseness from a rough

surface (a number in the hundreds) for removing large areas of waste to ultra-fine gradients (a number in the thousands) that are useful for polishing and are useful for cleaning canopies and especially rough paint surfaces. These products also have a degree of flexibility and so are especially useful on curved or awkward areas. They can be purchased either from model shops or from the beauty product ranges of most shops and online retailers.

Left, below left and below right: *Fuselage being clipped from the sprue, ensuring the clippers are not actually in contact with the part. The sprue nub is then sanded down with a coarse sanding stick before being polished smooth with a fine-grade sanding stick.*

GLUES

Now that we have established what the models are made from and have trimmed and cleaned the parts, it's time to start sticking things together. For this we'll need to ensure we are matching the correct bonding agent to the right material. Very broadly speaking, the most commonly encountered glues are PVA, superglue, cement and solvent. PVA is a sticky paste and fine for attaching foliage and netting to models, but is not much use beyond that.

Superglue, or cyanoacrylate to give it its proper name, is a rapid-curing cement that bonds most materials. Given the rapidity of the bonding process, superglue works best when used in small controlled areas. I tend to apply it with a cocktail stick or equivalent, and apply small dabs to each part that will be bonded. It's best to get the parts joined and then come back and carefully add more superglue if you feel the bond needs it rather than flooding an area that will take forever to dry and potentially make a terrible mess of your model too.

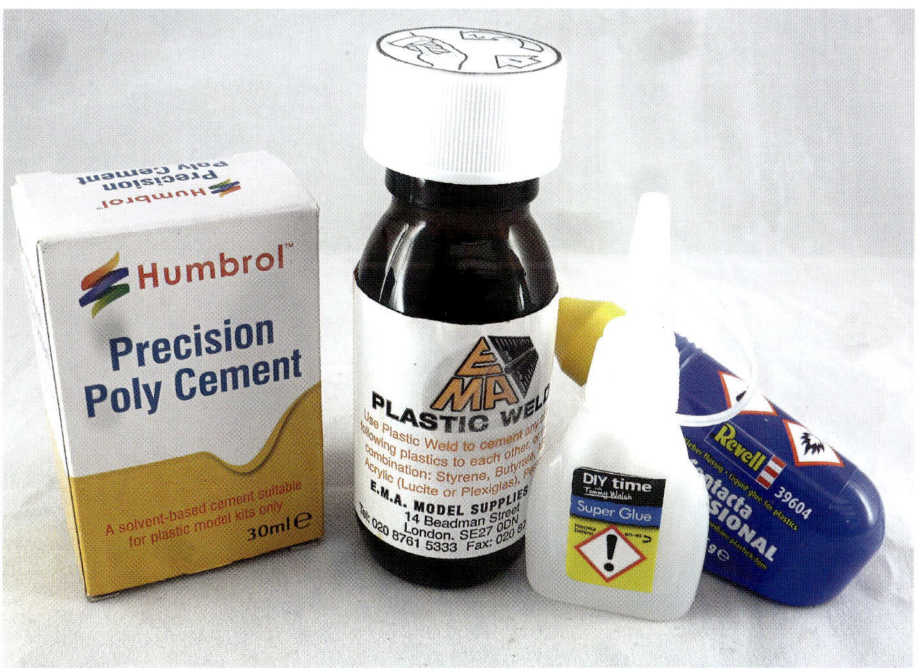

Adhesives for plastics such as those from Revell, Tamiya and Humbrol are all solvent-based to varying degrees and have a fairly wide range of drying times. In addition, there are also solvents designed with modelling in mind such as Plastic Weld, which are far more potent products. All of these, however, function off the basis of partially melting the two bonding surfaces of plastic into a very strong bond. They won't, however, bond metal, resin or plastic to metal or resin. For this you will still need superglue.

Finally we have cements. These typically come supplied in tubes and are very sticky and foul-smelling. While eventually they can give a decent bond, they are for the most part quite inferior to the purpose-designed adhesives already mentioned and should probably be avoided.

It's also worth checking the drying times for various glues. Superglue can have an activator that will speed up the drying times for when you need an even quicker bond. Alternatively, especially when working with small parts, a gel-type glue is very good as this will hold the part in place and also allow you to adjust positioning and fit.

FILLER

Gaps are something of an inevitability when working with multipart kits. If you are just starting out in the hobby and want to get the hang of just getting a kit finished they can be ignored; however, for best practice they will require cleaning up. Seams are another issue. These are the visible join lines between parts although they aren't gaps as such, and they can be somewhat unsightly. Fortunately, they are easy to remove if you wish.

If you do decide to fill the seams and gaps, then either model filler or superglue are good options to eliminate these issues. Superglue is a good tool for removing seams along fuselage spines and noses, especially as it can be sanded, polished and scribed easily, and has the added benefit of reinforcing the join at the same time.

Model filler is pretty easy to find in most brick and mortar hobby shops, and is widely manufactured by Humbrol, Revell, Vallejo and the like. Filler is very easy to use simply by squeezing a bit of filler onto some card and then applying some to the necessary area with a cocktail stick. Once dry, it's easily sanded with files or wet-and-dry paper. Most fillers take a few hours to dry before they are ready to be sanded and shaped.

This fuselage join has had the seam filled with superglue and was then polished smooth.

Acrylic fillers such as that produced by Vallejo can be applied to a gap, allowed to set for forty-five minutes or so and then removed with a damp cotton bud or allowed to fully harden and then sanded with files or wet-and-dry paper. All these types of filler essentially perform the same job; however, the acrylic ones tend to be more forgiving.

Sometimes filler is not enough to deal with a larger gap. These can still be treated with filler; however, adding a wedge of plasticard to the gap, trimming to make it flush with the surface of the model and then polishing the repair with fine wet-and-dry paper will give far better results.

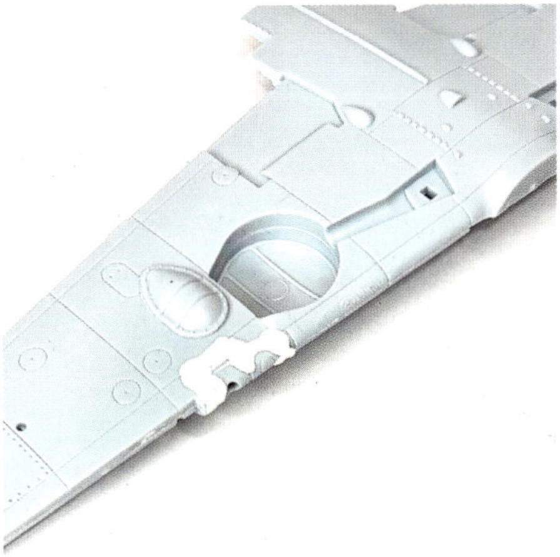

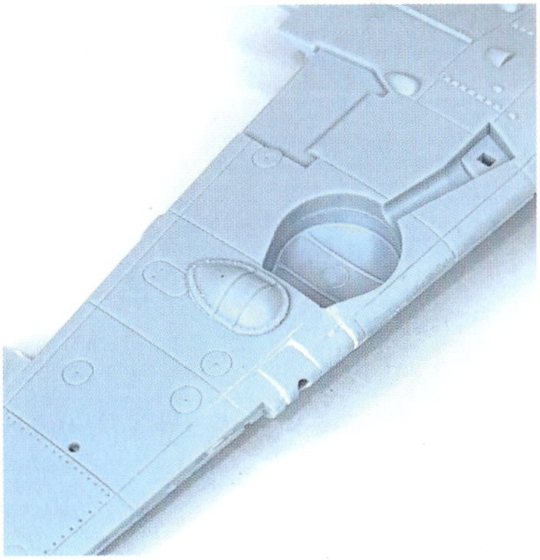

Above left and above right: *A plasticard wedge has been fitted into the gap before the excess is cut free and sanded smooth.*

SCRIBING DETAIL

When sanding parts it is easy to lose detail such as panel lines. To reinstate a panel line, you can use a scribe tool guided by some thick tape to guide the scribe along the required panels. A scribe is essentially a metal spike that you can use to score the kit plastic and reintroduce lost detail.

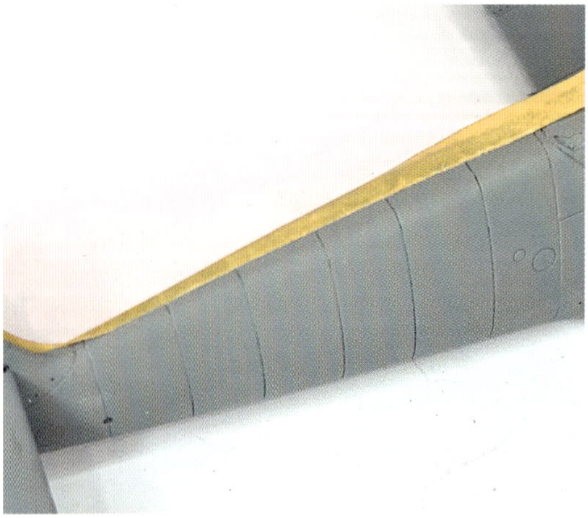

Left, opposite above left and opposite above right: *1) The fuselage spine is marked out with tape along the fuselage. 2) The spine seam has been rescribed and the surface polished. 3) The model has been primed to unify the surface finish for painting.*

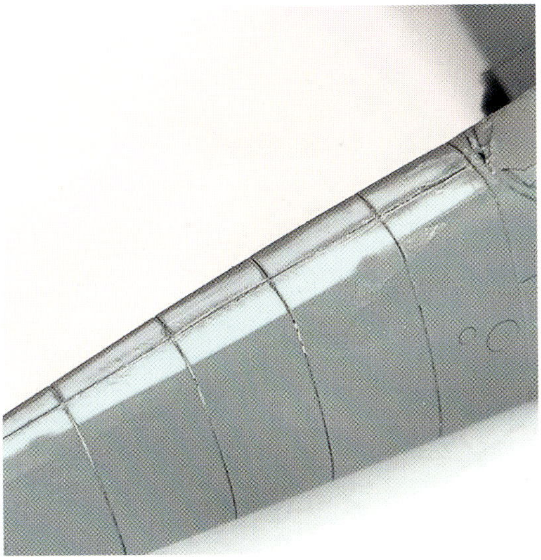

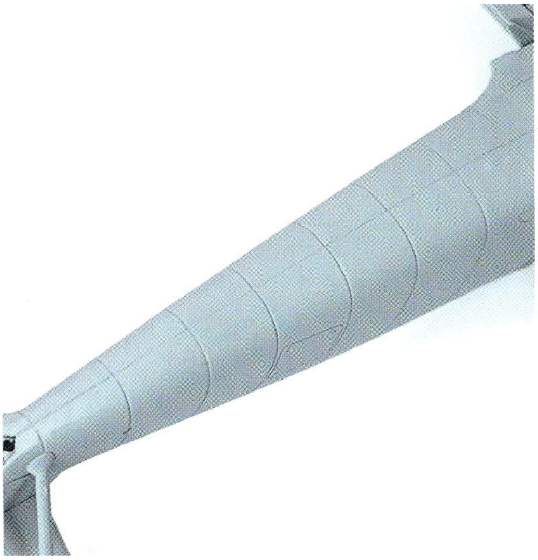

PAINT SHOP

Now that our model is built, we can start to paint it. Before we can look at some techniques though, I should probably cover a few key types of paint and paint products on the market. Before this though, it's best practice to give your models a wash in warm soapy water to remove any release agents, dust and finger grease etc. that can build up on the model and potentially harm the finish.

All the following guides in this book will be painted over primed models, and for most of these I'll be using a grey or black primer as covered in the specific text.

First of all, primers are probably the most important type of paint you can get, especially when working with resin or metal components. These differ from paint in being specially formulated to give a hard-wearing coat that gives a resilient surface for handling and painting. With most popular modelling paints, especially at the entry level of the hobby, being water-based acrylics, repeated handling without a primer can cause paint to wear off a finished model. Primers typically come in black, white, grey and dark red, and I prefer to get them from places selling car body paints.

Priming grey is an excellent way to view the model for any imperfections or fit issues, and will allow you to do any necessary remedial work. Often I'll give a light coat of grey primer, even if I'll also be applying a black layer as well.

Priming black or using black as your initial or base paint layer allows you to build up a greater degree of colour modulation and depth of tone. It's ideally used as part of an airbrushed paint scheme as the fine paint atomization allows strength of tone to gradually build up with each pass of the airbrush.

White and red primers are less useful for our purposes. White is generally a little too pale and bright, and can lead to tones looking a little washed out, while red is a more complex colour for the majority of our painting. That being said, if painting an RAF aircraft in trainer yellow, a red primer base would be a sensible decision as it would give the yellow a warmer tone and prevent it appearing green.

By far the most popular medium of paint used for modelling is acrylic. These are generally although not always water-soluble, but are quick-drying and hard-wearing. Most paint when purchased requires some thinning to get the best results as paint that is too thick will not only be difficult to get where you want it to go, but it may also swamp the detail on your model too. To thin your paint, simply apply a little of it to a pallet (an old tile or plastic lid is great for this), and then add an equal amount of water and stir together using an old brush. It's worth doing a little research into reviews of the paint range you are interested in using as you will find some good advice online regarding which thinners work best with the paints and whether they are more suitable for brush or airbrush application. Notable paint ranges can be found from Humbrol, AK Interactive, MIG AMMO, Tamiya, Revell and Humbrol.

For best results add a tiny amount of flow improver, especially if your chosen paint does not require a specific type of thinner. This will hold the coverage of the paint together well while still keeping the paint controllable. It's hard to give any ratio of paint to water as it depends on the paints you have, the brands and even the colours used.

When mixing paint for airbrushing, you will need to mix the paint a little thinner. As a rough guide, you will want an approximately 50/50 mix of paint to thinner, although this varies between both paint range and individual paint. If your paint range has its own brand of thinner, I'd also suggest using this to mix with the paint for airbrushing rather than using pure water as it will ensure that the paint flows as intended. With airbrushing, it is always recommended to experiment on some spare plastic to get a better idea of how the paint will perform before committing it to the model.

Enamel paints are oil-based, and while prevalent as paints in their own right are now largely used for weathering products. These have longer drying times than acrylics, but also allow you to work with them and blend them using mineral spirits.

Finally, oil paints are very useful for weathering. They can be thinned using mineral spirits or white spirit. It's recommended to use them in a well-ventilated area. They have a longer drying time than enamels, and can be reactivated several days after they have been applied to a model. This makes them ideal for subtle weathering effects as we will see later throughout this book.

PAINTBRUSHES AND CARE

As with most tools, brushes vary between super cheap where you get a pack of a dozen brushes for a few pounds up to fine Kolinsky sable brushes that can seem hugely expensive by comparison. Speaking as someone who paints a huge number of models, it's worth splashing out on the best quality brushes you can afford as not only will they last longer, they will work out cheaper in the long run.

To illustrate this, I've had some expensive brushes that are used pretty much every day for long periods, still very functional if now a bit worn. I also have a steady stream of cheaper brushes that seem to last a few months before being relegated to just mixing and stirring purposes.

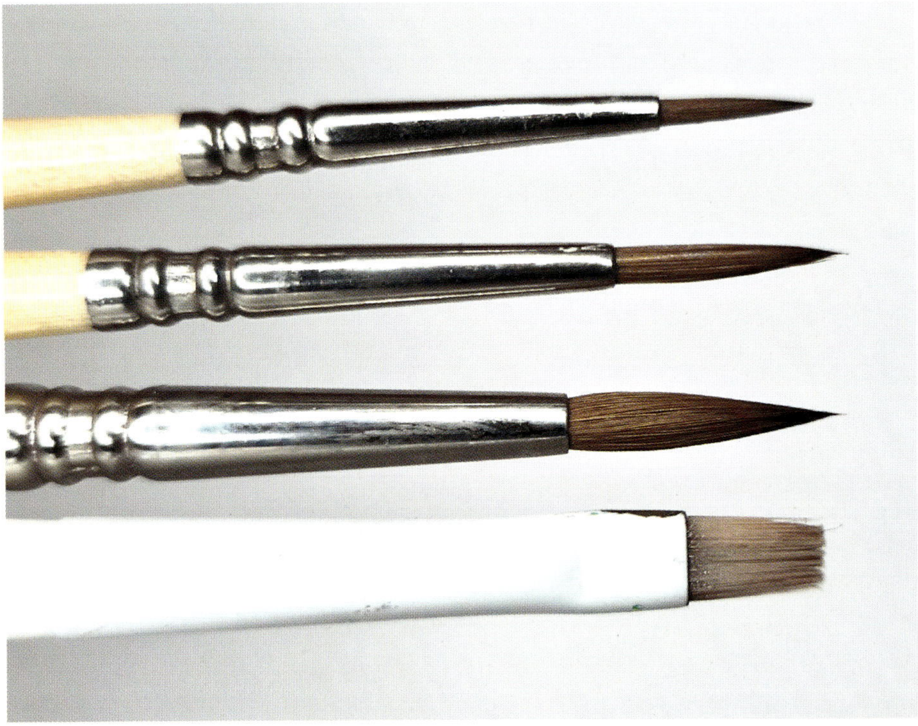

A high-quality brush will also give you better brush control and a finer finish. Personally I predominantly use the Winsor & Newton series 7, Rosemary & Co. and Broken Toad ranges. That said, for things like applying washes and dry brushing, I do find simple, cheap hobby brushes from the craft shop to be perfectly adequate. For less expensive but still serviceable brushes, Pro Arte, Army Painter and Games Workshop all produce useful examples. Again though, it's worth also having some cheap disposable brushes for jobs like mixing paint, applying washes, dry brushing and applying glue, anything for which you do not want to use your best brushes.

Paintbrushes themselves are typically made either from synthetic weave or natural hair. Synthetic brushes don't tend to hold paint as well as natural brushes; however, when working with acrylic paint this isn't too much of a hindrance as you will be cleaning the brush anyway thanks to the rapid drying times of the paint. Natural brushes tend to give you better control over the application of paint and they are better at retaining their point for precision application and also hold more paint, giving the added benefit of being able to keep working on a subject for longer. Natural fibre bristles are at their best when used for detail work, especially painting areas such as faces or fine layered highlights.

As you work, you will naturally need to clean your brush. When using most acrylic paints a simple pot of water will be sufficient for use between changing colours and to prevent paint drying in the bristles, and regardless of what your brush's bristles are made from I'd not recommend leaving it any longer than a few minutes before giving it a quick swish around in some water. You can add a little washing-up liquid to your water too, although I've not found this necessary myself.

For more long-term care, there is a wide range of brush cleaners and conditioners on the market, and frequently there are products put out from each of the major paint ranges. It's worth investing in either some brush cleaner or better yet some brush soap to prevent excess wear or damage to your brushes' bristles. Odourless brush cleaner can be especially handy to aid restoring brushes. Each of these products will have its own set of specific instructions usually printed on the side of the packaging, typically involving giving the brush a solid swishing around in the cleaner/soap, leaving it to stand for a bit and then rinsing clean and shaping. I've used a combination of brush soap and high-end sable brushes to keep the same fine brushes in use almost every day for several years now!

Regarding which size and shape of brush you should be getting, a size 0, size 1, size 2 and a size 4 round should be sufficient. Though it may seem counter-intuitive, a brush with a good quality point and fairly long bristles will be far more useful and give a much better result for fine detail work than a very tiny brush as the paint will dry too quickly on the small brush to be of much use in precision painting.

You'll probably spot in the painting guides the use of flat brushes as well as make-up brushes. These are just what they sound like: either flat chisel-like brushes or round, dense short-haired brushes. These are both great for dry brushing as they have a good amount of control and lend themselves well to pulling over the raised detail, allowing you to have fairly precise highlights quickly. They aren't compulsory for dry brushing, but they do make life a lot easier.

VARNISH

A varnish is a clear protective layer applied to the model to protect the paint finish during handling. Varnishes are essentially gloss, matt or satin in finish. Gloss is very shiny, matt is very flat and satin is somewhere in between, and it largely depends on the manufacturer as to whereabouts it falls between the two. Whether you use just one type of varnish, both types or none at all is entirely up to you.

Varnishes can be obtained in many forms, but most useful for our purposes are those in spray cans. These allow you to varnish many models quickly and evenly, and also have the added bonus of generally being touch-dry reasonably quickly. Avoid spraying on hot or humid days, however, as this can cause the paint to cloud and potentially ruin your paint job!

Hopefully these tips and techniques will have you feeling confident about getting on with assembling and painting your models, and as ever should be treated as just a stepping-off point for your own experiments. Now on to actually building your models!

2

RAF Day Fighters

There can be few more iconic paint schemes applied to a combat aircraft than the Dark Earth, Dark Green and Sky applied to RAF fighters during the Battle of Britain period. In this chapter we will have a brief overview of the RAF during the battle, as well as the camouflage and markings used by them immediately before, during and after the battle.

We shall then proceed to build and paint a pair of Spitfires, as well as adding some simple additional detailing that can really elevate the finesse of your model. One aircraft will be brush-painted while the second will be painted using an airbrush.

When the Battle of Britain officially began on 10 July 1940, the Royal Air Force had been in a process of rapid modernization, integrating high-performance monoplane fighter aircraft with a system of detection, command and control, and logistical support.

During the 1930s most air forces' standard doctrine had been that 'The bomber always gets through.' This thinking ran that as multi-engined bomber aircraft were, at the time, technologically advanced combining high-speed and low-drag all-metal designs, they would be able to outrun the enemy as well as being harder to shoot down with the limited machine-gun armaments of contemporary fighters.

In Britain this thinking was challenged by Air Chief Marshal Sir Hugh Dowding. Dowding was placed in command of the newly formed Fighter Command. While bringing in high-performance fighter aircraft and well-trained crews as a major part of the defence of Great Britain was a key part of the later success of Fighter Command, what really gave the Royal Air Force the edge was the Dowding System.

The Dowding System was the first fully integrated air defence system in the world using a combination of radar and observation posts to track and monitor formations of enemy aircraft, and then vectoring fighters to intercept from a position of advantage. In addition to the fighters, the system also controlled ground defences as well such as searchlights, anti-aircraft guns and barrage balloons.

Fighter Command was split into four geographical groups: 10 Group in the south-west of England as well as Wales, 11 Group covering London and the south-east, 12 Group covering the rest of the east of England, the Midlands and parts of the north, and finally 13 Group covering the rest of northern England, Scotland and Northern Ireland. These commands would each receive the intelligence from Bentley Priory, the centralized control point, and would in turn feed the information to relevant sector station airfields, which could then initiate a scramble and get their fighters in the air with enough time to achieve their height, speed and position.

Between routine patrols and scrambles, these fighters could be airborne several times a day, especially those squadrons operating in 11 Group, placing a high degree of strain on the pilots and machines based there.

In May 1940, the German blitzkrieg in the west saw the RAF heavily engaged against the Luftwaffe as well as German ground targets. Bomber Command especially suffered staggering losses during the campaign; however, the pilots also gained valuable experience.

Following the Fall of France in June 1940, the next month was spent making ready for the huge clashes that would be occurring through the rest of the summer.

As the German invasion barges and bomber fleets were massing across the Channel, the Royal Air Force was also making preparations. Some 2,937 pilots are officially credited as having flown with at least one operation sortie, and those with an average age of just 20. These pilots, while mostly British, also included 574 pilots from 16 countries. Most numerous of these were Poles, although New Zealanders, Czechs and Canadians as well as pilots from numerous other countries from the all over the world served together. Indeed, the commander of 11 Group, Air Vice Marshal Sir Keith Park was a New Zealander.

It should also be noted that fifty-seven Fleet Air Arm pilots served in the Battle of Britain, pilots serving both in their own Squadrons 804 and 808 as well as serving with RAF units. A little outside the scope of this book, they would typically be using Gloster Gladiators within their own units and were notably stationed to protect the Royal Naval base at Scapa Flow.

The two most important aircraft types operated during the battle by Fighter Command were the Hawker Hurricane and the Supermarine Spitfire. That said, also in use were the Boulton Paul Defiant, the Bristol Blenheim, the Gloster Gladiator and later the Bristol Beaufighter. The Westland Whirlwind was also available, although this particular type was kept in reserve should an invasion occur.

A Blenheim Mk I. This aircraft, L1295, served with several squadrons and most likely served during the Battle of Britain before being written off in an accident in 1943. This picture, probably taken in late 1939 or early 1940, appears to have had the fuselage roundel and codes at least partially obscured. **(Kent Battle of Britain Museum Collection)**

A fine portrait of a Defiant in day-fighter colours. Although we can't see any identifying codes, the photograph does demonstrate the black framing on the turret well. **(Kent Battle of Britain Museum Collection)**

The Hawker Hurricane first flew on 6 November 1935 and was developed as the need for high-performance monoplanes became unavoidable. Designed by Sydney Camm, the Hurricane was in many ways an evolution of the Hawker Company's biplane fighters and shared many similar design features. Indeed, early variants had a fabric-covered wing and all variants had a fabric-covered rear fuselage and tailplane. By the time of the Battle of Britain, most of the Hurricanes in service had metal wings.

While a little slower than the Spitfire and Messerschmitt Bf 109, the Hurricane was extremely tough, could and did operate anywhere in the world and was heavily armed. Initially armed with eight .303 Browning machine guns in the Mk I, versions introduced after the Battle of Britain would be armed with twelve machine guns or four 20mm cannon, bombs, rockets or even 40mm anti-tank guns.

The Hurricane was the most numerous fighter operated by Fighter Command during the battle and the 1,715 Hurricanes succeeded in shooting down approximately 656 enemy aircraft, more than any other air or ground defence system.

The only Victoria Cross awarded to a Fighter Command pilot during the battle, and also during the Second World War, was that of James Brindley Nicolson of 249 Squadron, who climbed back into his burning aircraft to successfully shoot down a further German aircraft. He survived the encounter despite being badly burned. He would continue flying with the RAF before being killed in 1945 when the aircraft in which he was travelling crashed at sea in the Bay of Bengal.

This 87 Squadron Hurricane shows two different styles of lettering on the fuselage coding, with the aircraft's individual code letter using a marginally thinner style. Also worth noting is the phrase 'Kia Ora' ('Be Well') under the cockpit. **(Kent Battle of Britain Museum Collection)**

The pilot of this Hurricane is wearing a white pre-war 'Prestige suit'. Additionally in this image we can see that the inside of the undercarriage door appears to be painted in Sky, and the guns have had a freshly applied red dope cover. **(Kent Battle of Britain Museum Collection)**

This Hurricane has a few interesting features. We can see a small painting of a cat just below the cockpit. On the wing is a rectangle of gas detection paint, which would change colour in the presence of poison gas. Also worth noting is the exhaust staining on the fuselage. **(Kent Battle of Britain Museum Collection)**

These 615 Squadron Hurricanes show a variety of weathering, with the aircraft on the right of the image showing signs of significant use. **(Kent Battle of Britain Museum Collection)**

The Supermarine Spitfire might very well be the most famous fighter aircraft of all time, certainly within Europe, and it has achieved truly legendary status, in no small part due to its role during the Battle of Britain.

Designed by R.J. Mitchell, and later Joseph Smith following Mitchell's untimely death, the Spitfire was designed according to the same requirement for a high-speed monoplane fighter as the Hurricane. First flying just four months after the Hurricane, the Spitfire was a radically different design being pretty much an all-metal construction with a thin but very strong elliptical wing. Through the more advanced design features of the aircraft, the Spitfire was fast, manoeuvrable and had an impressive rate of climb while carrying the same eight machine-gun armament as the Hurricane.

The design of the Spitfire would prove to be extremely adaptable, with more than 20,000 aircraft being produced in both land-based and carrier versions as well as two major engine variations, the Merlin and the Griffon, and the aircraft saw considerable post-war service as well.

Entering service in 1938 with No. 19 Squadron at RAF Duxford, the Spitfire's finest hour was during the Battle of Britain in which around 800 of them would serve. The Spitfire proved to be extremely successful, often with a flight of just three aircraft engaging many more times their number of enemy aircraft yet coming out of the engagement victorious.

Above: ***A 66 Squadron Spitfire in late 1939 or early 1940. These aircraft demonstrate the national insignia in use prior to the Battle of Britain.*** **(Kent Battle of Britain Museum Collection)**

Right: ***A Spitfire being refuelled by an Albion refueller, a process that could be completed very quickly.*** **(Kent Battle of Britain Museum Collection)**

This Spitfire demonstrates signs of significant wear and tear on the wing root, as well as a small piece of personal art forward of the cockpit hatch. **(Kent Battle of Britain Museum Collection)**

While most RAF aircraft had individual serial codes painted in black, some aircraft such as this Spitfire had their codes painted in dark grey. **(Kent Battle of Britain Museum Collection)**

The standard Royal Air Force camouflage pattern on the upper surfaces of aircraft featured a brown and green disruptive pattern. Dark Earth was used for the brown areas and this was a mid-brown colour. It's worth noting that RAF ground vehicles operating in the southern areas of Britain were also repainted this colour from their RAF blue. The green part of the pattern is a dark green with a touch of olive to its appearance. This colour is sometimes interpreted as having quite a blue tone, especially in some premixed model paints; however, this is incorrect.

These disruptive patterns were applied at the factory, using masking templates to create set patterns. Two forms were used, the Type A and Type B pattern, and these were a mirror of one another. On Hurricanes, the Type A pattern was applied to aircraft with odd numbered serial codes while the Type B was applied to aircraft with even number codes. On Spitfires, however, Type A was applied to aircraft with even serials and Type B on aircraft with the odd numbers. However, even this is not entirely consistent and some variation occurred.

Underside colours were a little more complicated. Prior to June 1940, RAF aircraft were painted white on the underside of their starboard wing and black under the port wing. This was intended to be split along the fuselage and also applied to the tail; however, some confusion occurred and some aircraft had their fuselage and possible tail areas painted aluminium instead.

In June 1940 the order was given to paint the undersides of aircraft in Sky. Sky was described to units as being a duck egg bluish-green. The paint for this, Sky Type S, would not be readily available for at least a month so individual squadrons were required to paint their aircraft using whatever approximation of this colour they could come up with following such a vague description.

Standardization would come; however, it can also be seen in period photos that there was some variation in tones as well. Interestingly some older aircraft display areas of black paint on gun maintenance hatches and the insides of undercarriage doors. This is particularly notable when the black paint is visible.

Spinners and propellers would generally be painted black, with yellow tips on the end of the propellers. However, some aircraft and squadrons may have used other colours, possibly on an individual basis.

In terms of insignia and markings, Royal Air Force aircraft tended to all be marked in largely the same way during the Battle of Britain. On the top of the wings were roundels of dark blue and deep red. Underneath the wings blue, white and red roundels were present. Similar roundels were also painted onto the fuselage sides; however, these also had a yellow outer ring around them. The colours of each ring of both these types of roundel were the same thickness.

Fin flashes on the tail of the aircraft had three vertical stripes with the red stripe towards the front of the aircraft, white in the centre and blue towards the tail. Thickness and shape could vary here, so it's worth checking your references for the particular aircraft or squadron you are modelling.

Each squadron would be assigned a two-letter code, and then each aircraft in the squadron would also have an individual letter assigned to it. As a couple of examples, 32 Squadron (Hurricanes) used GZ as their squadron code, so an aircraft could have the code GZ A.

Generally a squadron would be split into four flights of three aircraft, and theoretically these would have corresponding letters assigned to their aircraft. An aircraft from 'A' Flight could be assigned the letters A, B or C. Machines from 'B' Flight could therefore be D, E or F. However, there was some discretion here, especially as aircraft availability and replacements meant that pilots would fly what was available and they were not assigned personal aircraft as such. These codes would be painted in a medium grey-toned paint.

Wheel wells and the inner faces of undercarriage doors would be painted with aluminium paint. However, this too was not set in stone as some aircraft, particularly Spitfires, appear to have had their wheel wells and undercarriage doors painted the colour of the underside of the aircraft.

Finally, individual aircraft serial numbers which served as registration numbers were painted at the rear of the fuselage in small letters and numbers, and were generally although not always in black.

Almost as iconic as the Supermarine Spitfire, within the model-making hobby there are few combinations more synonymous with the hobby in the UK than an Airfix Spitfire so we will be building two in this chapter. The first will be a 1/72 scale kit that will be brush-painted and a 1/48 scale model that will be airbrushed.

The 1/72 scale model will be built to represent Spitfire DW-K P9495 of 610 Squadron. This aircraft features in some of the most famous photos of the battle, especially those of the aircraft at RAF Hawkinge. It seems a fitting subject, therefore, for the first build of this guide. P9495 was taken on strength with 610 Squadron in early June 1940, flying numerous sorties between June and July. In July, while being flown by Sergeant Stanley John Arnfield, P9495 was attacked by a pair of Messerschmitt 109s and badly damaged. Sergeant Arnfield was able to return the damaged aircraft to base; however, it was written off as being damaged beyond repair.

Sergeant Arnfield was an experienced pilot having joined the Royal Air Force in 1930 and transferring to flight training in 1937. In 1938 he transferred to 610 Squadron, transitioning to flying Spitfires. No. 610 Squadron and Sergeant Arnfield flew in the Battle of France and assisted in covering the Dunkirk evacuation. Arnfield would continue to fly in the Battle of Britain, being shot down again on 24 August 1940. He was able to successfully bail out of his aircraft, spending some time in hospital as a consequence. He would go on to survive the war, transferring to Bomber Command and flying Lancaster bombers. He died in 1954.

For the 1/48 scale model, we will be building a representation of Spitfire ZD F P9323 of 222 Squadron. The aircraft appears to have been accepted into service with 222 Squadron in mid-March 1940, and most likely took part in the Dunkirk operation before the squadron was moved north for a rest period. In August 1940, 222 Squadron along with Spitfire P9323 moved south again, joining 11 Group and being stationed at RAF Hornchurch.

On 30 August, P9323 was being flown by Sergeant Arthur William Peter Spears when he was engaged by several Messerschmitt 109s and shot down. Sergeant Spears managed to bail out successfully, spending the rest of the day at RAF Eastchurch where he was also caught up in an air raid the following day. His aircraft crashed near a farm near Minster on the Isle of Sheppey.

Spears would continue flying until April 1941, when he was shot down by German ace Adolf Galland. He would again successfully bail out, although he received wounds to his right arm and leg. Spears survived the war, serving in a variety of roles both on the ground and in the air, and eventually retired from the RAF in 1970 having attained the rank of squadron leader. He died in September 1998.

Above left: *This wing panel shows a rarely seen detail of the inside face of one of the gun bay covers of a Battle of Britain era Spitfire. This aircraft, coded N3120, served briefly with 266 Squadron and was being flown by Wing Commander Ian Gleed when it broke up during a test flight. Gleed would survive the crash, although he died in 1943.* **(Kent Battle of Britain Museum Collection)**

Above right: *This small chip of light blue paint demonstrates a very interesting variation in the underside colour used on RAF aircraft during the period, being distinctly bluer than the typical RAF Sky paint. The section of lower wing present here was recovered from Hurricane P2728 flown by George James Drake. Drake served with 607 Squadron and was lost with this aircraft on 9 September 1940.* **(Kent Battle of Britain Museum Collection)**

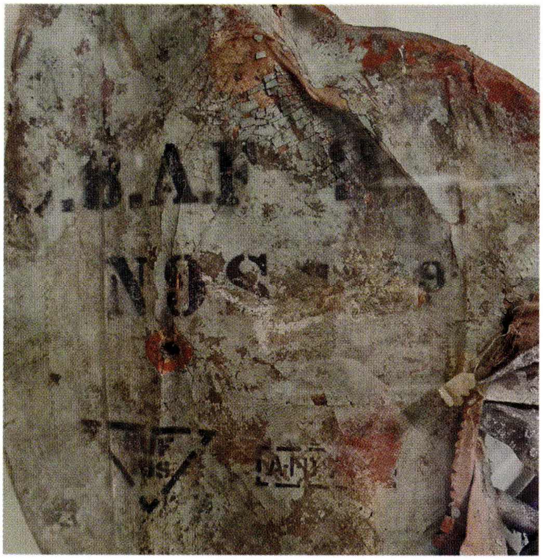

Above left and above right: *Both these pictures show pieces of wreckage recovered from Spitfire P7303. The first demonstrates the Sky paint used on the under surfaces of RAF aircraft, along with the red linen doping used on canvas areas to seal and strengthen them prior to painting. The second picture is a good example of the Interior Green paint used on RAF aircraft as well as part of a harness. Spitfire P7303 served with 616 Squadron, and was being flown by Pilot Officer Peter Chesters when he was shot down on 27 October 1940. He would survive the Battle of Britain, although he died later in the war.* **(Kent Battle of Britain Museum Collection)**

This seat was recovered from the remains of Spitfire P9458. Here we can see the seat cushion, as well as remnants of the Interior Green paint. P9458 was flown by Flying Officer Oswald St John Pigg of 72 Squadron, who was killed in this aircraft on 1 September 1940. **(Kent Battle of Britain Museum Collection)**

Above left: *This section of Spitfire was recovered from a marsh in the 1970s and has retained a remarkable amount of its original paint. This gives us a good understanding not only of the colours, but also the sharp edge of the camouflage patterns. Spitfire R6713 served with 65 Squadron and was being flown by Flying Officer Franciszek Gruszka when he was shot down and killed on 18 August 1940.* **(Kent Battle of Britain Museum Collection)**

Above right: *This Spitfire wing, although showing some fading and weathering, gives us a rare appreciation of original wartime paint with the remains of the roundel and camouflage still visible. The wing also demonstrates the hard edge of the camouflage pattern as well as how flush the rivets were on the wing surfaces. Spitfire X4273, coded XT-K, was being flown by Flying Officer Robin McGregor Waterston when he was shot down and killed.* **(Kent Battle of Britain Museum Collection)**

AIRFIX 1/72 SPITFIRE

To start the builds in this book, we will begin with probably the most stereotypically well-known model kit, at least in Europe, the Airfix 1/72 Spitfire Mk I. While the techniques here are being used on a Spitfire, they can be used on any early war RAF aircraft as the techniques and colours are largely consistent across all of them, regardless of scale or the type being modelled.

This is a very simple to construct kit and ideal for a beginner to the hobby. We will be brush-painting this particular model and modelling it standing on its undercarriage. We'll leave the pilot out, but add some simple seat belts as a little bit of easy extra detailing.

1) Initial assembly

The first thing one should always do when building a kit is to read through the instructions and ensure that you understand how different assembly and detail options apply to your chosen subject. Some kits give options for open panels, different flap positions and even alternative versions with different features found on the full-size aircraft.

As this kit is very simple, all we have to do is decide whether to build with wheels up or down and with or without a pilot figure. As mentioned already, we're doing the aircraft wheels down and without a pilot. When one is more experienced at building kits, you can go through a build and start picking out sub-assemblies out of sequence of the build instructions to work on and speed up a build. For now though, we will simply follow the sequence of the kit's build.

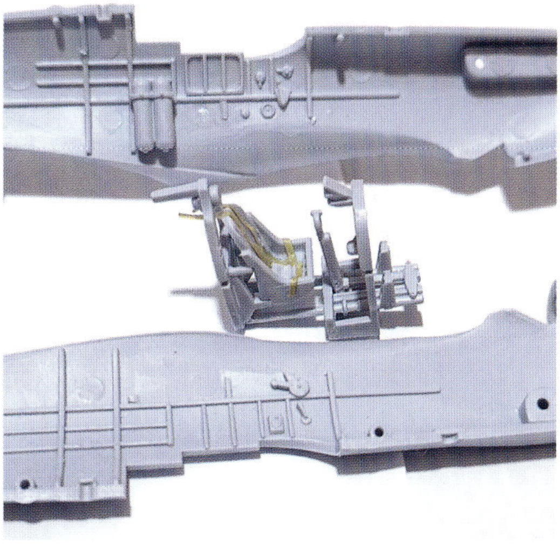

We'll do the initial steps, building up the interior parts but not sealing the fuselage together yet. Build the cockpit tub, then let it all dry ready for paint. We can also build the propeller assembly, although we won't be adding it to the model for a while. If you wish, you can add seat belts to the pilot's seat. These are simply done by cutting some strips of masking tape to an appropriate length for the seat and using the adhesive properties of the masking tape to attach them. To make the joint permanent, use a cocktail stick to run a small bead of superglue along the edge of the belts.

2) Interior painting

In 1940 the majority of RAF aircraft, especially fighters, had their interiors painted in a light grey-green named Interior Green; however, some parts could be painted aluminium. The Hurricane, for example, has a distinctive interior framework that in this period was in the aluminium colour and the Spitfire's fuselage aft of the rear bulkhead was also aluminium. All fighter aircraft had switches and tools around the inside of the cockpit, and these would typically be painted black, but may have some red or yellow switches. It's worth checking references or the instructions if you want to pick these out, and on this model we will be.

We'll be using acrylic paints from the Humbrol range for this build as they are good quality and easy to use. When working with acrylics, it's worth giving plastic components a wash with water and washing-up liquid to help adhesion. Alternatively you can give the parts a spray with a can of primer paint. Many such paints are available, both modelling and automotive. I'd recommend a spray from a model company, however, as you can be confident of getting a finer finish. Humbrol and Citadel (Warhammer) sprays would be my personal recommendation. I've sprayed these parts grey before applying base coats to help the adhesion of the paint. It's always worth letting one colour dry before moving on to the next to prevent any paint bleeding into another.

As these are acrylics they are touch-dry in minutes so this doesn't cause too much of a delay in building. Thin the paints until they flow nicely from your brush, and be aware that you may need more than one coat, waiting for the paint to dry between each application. We have also picked out some switches in appropriate reds and yellows. It's also worth painting the undercarriage areas of the model now, and adding the definition should you wish to.

Area	Brush used	Paint used
Fuselage sides, seat and floor	Size 2 round	Humbrol 78 Interior Green
Detail parts, seat cushion, instrument panel	Size 1 round	Humbrol 33 Matt Black
Aft fuselage, oxygen bottles, wheel wells	Size 1 round	Humbrol 56 Aluminium
Seat belts	Size 1 round	Humbrol 72 Khaki Drill
Undercarriage doors, wheel wells, wheel hubs and undercarriage legs	Size 2 round	Humbrol 56 Aluminium
Tyres	Size 1 round	Matt Black

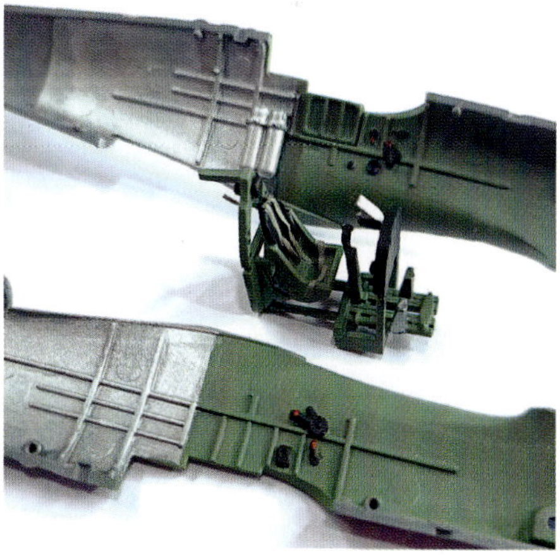

3) Adding definition (optional)

This is an optional step; however, it can make a big difference to the appearance of the model. We will be mixing a wash of thinned dark green paint and using this to add some definition to the detail areas of the model. You could use a black or dark brown; however, in this scale the contrast will be too stark. Instead we will be mixing some of the Interior Green paint and some of the dark green we will be using as part of the aircraft's camouflage colours and then thinning this down.

To mix the paint, we will apply equal amounts of paint using the dropper of the pot to our palette. As the area we will be painting is pretty small, you will only need one to two drops of each colour. Once the colour is thoroughly mixed, add around as much water as you have paint and then carefully apply the wash into any detail. Capillary action should help the wash flow into and around any details. Any overspill can be cleaned up by using a clean brush to simply soak up the excess paint.

You could use a pre-mixed green wash from one of many paint ranges or buy a different green paint to mix your own washes. However, for the purposes of this guide I'll be assuming the builder does not have access to a large selection of paints. Once this is done, you can also add the instrument panel decal if you wish. Further details on decals will be covered more fully further into the book.

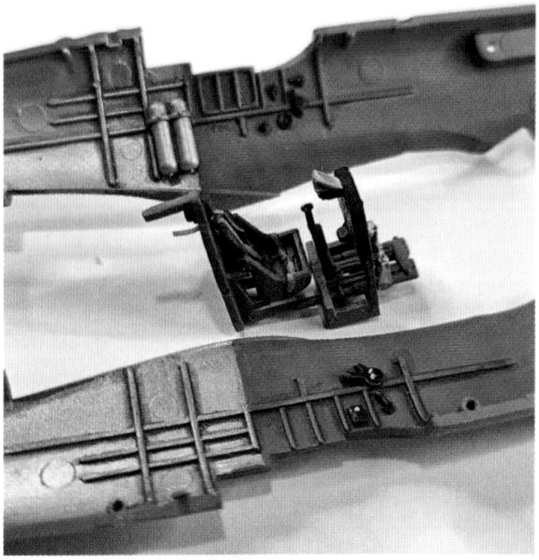

Area	Brush used	Paint used
Moulded details	Size 2 round	Humbrol 78 Interior Green + Humbrol 116 US Dark Green + water

4) Building the airframe

Now we will fit the cockpit into the fuselage and seal the halves together. If you want the propeller to spin, follow the instructions on how to assemble this, being careful with glue. However, I generally find it complicates the painting and handling process so I prefer to glue the propeller on once the model is complete.

You may find a seam along the top of the fuselage. If you want to remove this, follow the suggestions for doing so in the tools chapter of this book.

Putting the fuselage to one side, we can now assemble the main wings. This will also require painting the wheel wells for the undercarriage. Again I've primed the model in grey, although this is not entirely necessary. I've picked them out in aluminium, although this can vary between different aircraft types. If you wish you can mix a dark wash using black paint or black and brown paint as detailed in the previous step and paint this into the details. You could also apply this to the undercarriage legs and doors at this stage as well. Don't forget to paint the inner part of the wing Interior Green as well as that forms the cockpit floor and will be visible.

I'd suggest painting the undercarriage parts on the sprue and leaving them off the model until the aircraft is being painted. Don't forget to paint the outside of the doors to match the underside of your model!

We will also be masking and adding the canopy, but use a specific canopy gluing product or a good PVA to attach this. You could add the canopy later; however, I find adding it before paint means that it looks like it's part of the airframe rather than just an attachment. Once the canopy is glued in place, paint the framing with Interior Green. This will

give the impression of the inside of the framing being painted the interior colours.

You can also add the various fittings on the underside of the aircraft at this point; however, I'd suggest leaving off the small delicate parts such as the tail wheel, pitot tube and antenna mast. You can leave those on the sprue for now. You may have a seam or gap at or around the wings and now is the time to fill that too, and then model is ready for painting.

This is another optional step, although I strongly recommend it. Using a can of spray grey primer, give the model a light coat which will serve two purposes. Firstly, it will unify the finish and highlight any flaws such as gaps, seams or other areas that you can choose to tidy up with a bit of sanding and filling. Secondly, the paint being applied to the model will key into the surface of it for a harder-wearing finish. This is particularly important when you are going to be masking and handling the model through the painting process.

Area	Brush used	Paint used
Whole model	Aerosol can	Grey primer

5) Paint Dark Earth

I find it much easier to paint the upper surfaces of the model first. The fuselage sides are easier to mask for working on the underside of the

aircraft, and it also prevents damage to the underside of the model's paint finish as you're working through the camouflage.

To apply the Dark Earth, we will thin the paint a little so that it flows better, and then using a medium-sized brush apply a neat, even coat over the model. The important thing here is for the paint to go on smoothly. Make sure the paint isn't running or pooling, and be careful it is not going on too thickly and clogging the detail. If the finish isn't particularly opaque, then you can let the previous layer of paint dry and apply another thin layer. It is infinitely better to allow the paint to slowly build up opacity in thin layers than to use one thick heavy layer that obscures detail.

Area	Brush used	Paint used
Upper surfaces of model	Size 3 or 4 round	Humbrol 29 Dark Earth

6) Outline the camouflage

We will now apply the disruptive pattern of the Dark Green. On the real aircraft these patterns were applied using mats to mask the necessary areas, and you can purchase pre-cut adhesive masks for applying the camouflage to your model.

We will look at applying your own masks to various patterns in later guides in this book, but for now we will be painting the pattern freehand. This may sound daunting, but is readily achievable.

Take a moment to look at the painting instructions for your model as these will show how the pattern was painted onto the aircraft. If you do not feel confident about painting the camouflage straight onto the model, you can use a pencil (ideally a water colour pencil) to draw the pattern in first.

Thin the paint so that it flows well and is controllable but is still a little translucent. Using a brush with a good point and decent well, paint the outline of the pattern across the aircraft. Let this dry, and then we will start filling in the pattern.

Area	Brush used	Paint used
Upper surfaces of model	Size 1 or 2 round	Humbrol 116 US Dark Green

7) Filling in the camouflage

Once you are happy with the sketched-in outline of the camouflage, you can start to fill in the pattern. Keeping the paint thinned to flow

smoothly, start building up the colour. Use several thin coats as needed to get the opacity required.

Area	Brush used	Paint used
Upper surfaces of model	Size 1 or 2 round	Humbrol 116 US Dark Green

8) Paint lower surfaces

I'd suggest leaving the model for twenty-four hours between painting the upper surface and the lower surface. I'd also suggest masking off the demarcation line between the upper and lower surfaces and 6mm Kabuki tape is ideal for this task.

We will now apply the Sky colour to the underside of the aircraft. As with applying paint to the upper surfaces, keep the paint thin and let the colour slowly build up in opacity. Be mindful that although you have masked along the edges, paint can still bleed under the tape. To avoid this, carefully paint up to the edge and then paint inwards, moving the brush away from the taped edge. Some paint may still bleed through, and you can rectify this by neatly painting the surface colour back onto the model once the tape is removed.

Area	Brush used	Paint used
Lower surfaces of model, undercarriage bay doors, tail wheel strut and pitot tube	Size 3 or 4 round	Humbrol 90 Sky

9) Finishing off

With the model painted, we can add the transfers and also add the small parts, the propeller and the undercarriage. This is a perfectly fine and respectable place to finish the model, especially if you want a clean, clear

Above and opposite: *The finished brush-painted Spitfire with transfers and weathering applied.*

representation of the type in your collection, although there are other steps you could add to the model if you wish.

Some weathering would give the model a more lived-in appearance, and a coat of flat or satin varnish would give the model a unified finish as some paints can dry with different degrees of sheen.

AIRFIX 1/48 SPITFIRE

For the 1/48 scale Spitfire we will be using a few more advanced techniques, including building an in-flight model, making homemade masks and airbrushing. The base kit is also more advanced, so some time will be needed to familiarize yourself with the instructions as to which parts are required and what trimming or fitting may be required to facilitate this.

1) Building the interior

We will be assembling this model with the pilot fitted, so it's important to check if any parts need omitting or removing during the assembly process. We'll build the cockpit into the following sub-assemblies: each fuselage side, the seat, the front bulkhead and instrument panel, the floor and the rear bulkhead. We will also build the pilot.

There are also a few parts indicated that need removing: these are the canopy rail for a closed cockpit and the rudder pedals, and these will be removed as indicated in the instructions.

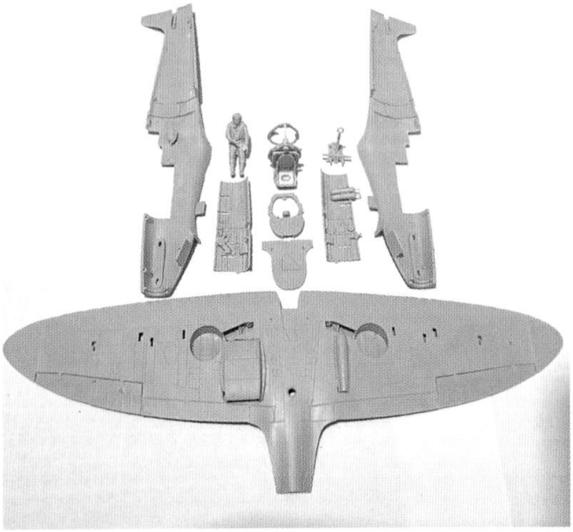

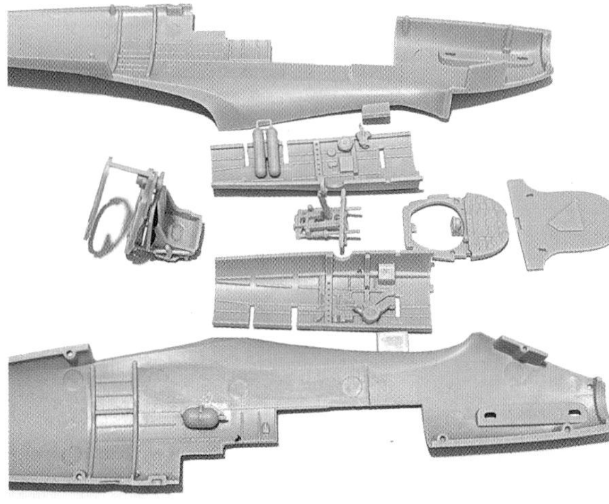

2) Painting the interior

While the colours and processes from the brush-painting would also work here using the airbrush techniques, we'll be doing something slightly different with this build. With this model we will be using a black primer to start with, and then airbrushing the Interior Green onto the interior parts of the model.

Apply a light coat of the green all over at first, misting the paint on lightly. Give that a few minutes to appear touch dry, and then start building up the paint by spraying it into recesses in the centre of panels and large areas, leaving the areas that would naturally be in shadow to be darker.

You can also spray the rear part of the fuselage silver during this stage, as well as the oxygen bottles and rear bulkhead. We can also pick out the interior detail parts: the switches, seat fitting, instrument panel and so on. We will also be painting the pilot at this stage, but as figure-painting is a set of skills in its own right, this will be covered in a later chapter. Finally, we will add the transfers to the instrument panel as well as picking out the relevant switches in red, yellow and silver. If you are building a Hawker Hurricane, be sure to paint the interior framing and floor silver.

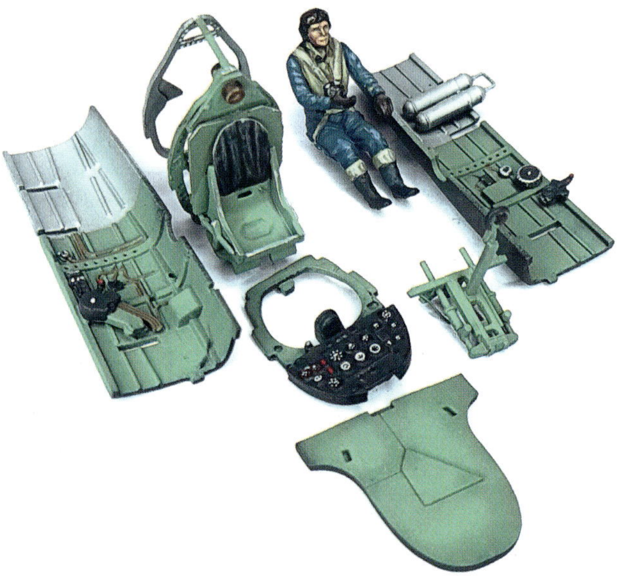

Area	Brush used	Paint used
Cockpit, seat, bulkheads, floor	Airbrush	Humbrol 78 Interior Green
Aft bulkhead, oxygen bottles, rear fuselage	Airbrush	Humbrol 56 Aluminium
Switches, seat cushion and detail parts	Size 1 or 2 round	Humbrol 33 Flat Black

3) Interior weathering (optional)

This is an optional step, and arguably not overly necessary with the pilot being installed as he will block most of the interior from sight; however, it will also be good practice.

To start with we will give the seat, floor, fuselage sides and seat bulkhead a light dry brushing with aluminium paint and this will replicate some light wear and chipping of the paint.

With the dry brushing in place, we use artist's oil paints to make a wash and apply this to the recesses and details. You could use acrylics too at this stage or a clay-based wash; however, oils are the simplest to clean up and the easiest to work with in my opinion.

Mix the oil paints with the appropriate thinners. You'll probably want a mix of around nine parts thinner to one part paint so the wash will be very thin. We're going to use a dark brown wash to simulate accumulated dirt and wear, although you could use a grey or dark green if you prefer. Allow the wash to flow into and around details, leave for an hour or two, and then by using an old brush dampened with thinners you can lift off any overspill or excess wash. The beauty of oils is that you will have a very long time to work with them should you change your mind about the appearance of the effect.

Area	Brush used	Paint used
Edges of panels, seat and floor	Small make-up or chisel	Humbrol 56 Aluminium
Recesses and details	Old size 2	Winsor & Newton Raw Umber

4) Interior assembly

Finally we can now bring all the interior sub-assemblies together. Be mindful that some joints may need paint removing by carefully scraping the paint away from the mating surfaces. It's worth using a needle-nosed

plastic cement for some parts or even a superglue to attach these parts. As ever, test fit everything until you are happy with how it assembles before committing to glue.

5) Further assembly

We can now start making some progress with getting the bulk of the model built. As this Spitfire is being built with its wheels up, we don't need to worry about painting the undercarriage areas, although it's worth still building the wing spars as they give the model some more strength.

If you were opting to model the aircraft with the gun bays open and the wheels down, you can spray them black and then paint them aluminium with the guns painted black and brass ammunition. You can

weather these as you like, although an oil wash as we used in the cockpit would enhance the finish nicely.

As you are putting the airframe together, ensure that all parts are thoroughly cleaned of any sprue attachment points and mould lines as these can cause parts to fit poorly. Equally, ensure that you spend some time checking that the fit is solid.

You can now build the majority of the aircraft including fitting the retracted undercarriage doors, but leave off any aerials, tail wheel and any other small delicate pieces. We'll leave the propeller off as well for ease of painting. Leave the canopy off at this stage too, as when we are doing any sanding work dust can easily get into the cockpit and be impossible to remove.

Once you are happy with the finish of the airframe and have cleaned up any seams and gaps to your satisfaction, give the model a coating of grey primer, but don't forget to paint the canopy framing Interior Green first. The grey primer will allow us to inspect the surface of the model for any last imperfections which we can deal with if necessary.

6) Dark Earth upper surface

Before applying any further paint, I added a light coating of black as a base from which to work up as this will give a richer finish to the airbrush work we will be doing.

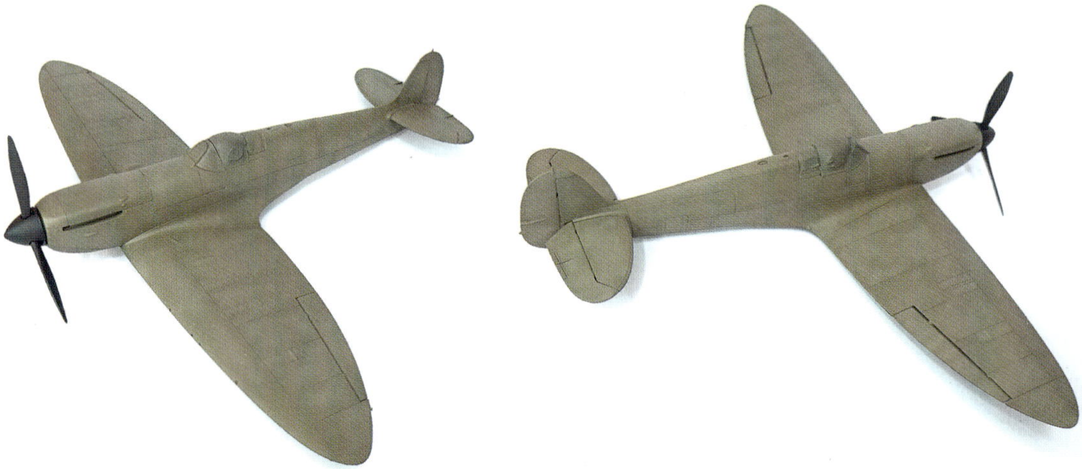

We will be applying the colours in the same sequence as we did when brush-painting the model, although using the airbrush to add a more subtly weathered finish to it.

To apply the Dark Earth, we will first of all mist on a light layer of Dark Earth. You are aiming to give the model an even fairly dark brown colour. Next, beginning by spraying away from the model, you will now aim to fill in each of its panels.

Carefully spray in each panel on the airframe, letting the paint slowly build up in opacity until you have an even colour with some shadow in the gaps between panels. While not overly realistic, it will give a nice effect of the stressed skin present on the real aircraft. If you wish to enhance this effect further, you can mix a little khaki into the Dark Earth to add some subtle variation in tone.

Area	Brush used	Paint used
Upper surfaces	Airbrush	Humbrol 29 Dark Earth

7) Masking

The Dark Green camouflage pattern on the real aircraft typically had an edge finish, especially when newly delivered from the factory.

Unfortunately this isn't really feasible to recreate with an airbrush without the aid of masking.

Once the Dark Earth has dried, I've masked out the pattern of the camouflage using some camouflage plastic putty from AK Interactive. You can use pre-cut masks for this or make your own using masking tape, but the masking putty can be recycled and used on further builds and is also less likely to pull or tear paint when you remove it from the model. However, masking tape is still superior when long straight lines are required.

With the putty, we will roll it into thin sausages and then apply them to the model forming the outlines of the camouflage pattern, using a cocktail stick to press and help shape the putty and press it to the surface of the model.

8) Dark Green camouflage

Once you are satisfied with the masking of the camouflage pattern, you can then begin spraying on the Dark Green. I'd recommend having a piece of plasticard or other card to test spraying before applying paint directly to the model to ensure that the paint is spraying with the desired finesse. Begin by applying light, misted coats onto the model. Too thick

an application will cause ridges to form against the masks. Again, you can mix some khaki into the Dark Green to add a little variation in tone to the camouflage. Once the camouflage is sprayed, you can simply peel off the putty and place it back in the pot to be reused at another time.

Area	Brush used	Paint used
Dark Green part of camouflage	Airbrush	Humbrol 116 US Dark Green

9) Sky undersides

After letting the model dry for around twenty-four hours, we will then mask off the upper surfaces with Kabuki masking tape and then spray the undersides. It's probably worth using some cheaper artist's masking tape to cover the rest of the upper surface of the model too as there is always a risk of overspray.

Again, we will mist the Sky on first and then fill in the individual panels, leaving a little shadow in the deeper panel areas. If the contrast is still a little stark, you can mist more of the Sky onto the model in light layers. Once finished, you can remove the masking tape and tidy up any chips or overspray and colour bleed with either a brush or an airbrush, it's entirely up to you.

When airbrushing you can sometimes get a slight orange peel or pebbling effect to the model's surface. This can cause problems with

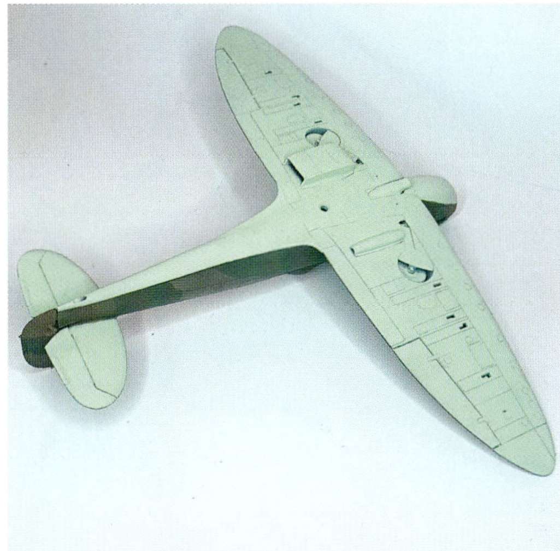

weathering and silvering of the transfers as we will discuss in more detail later.

For now, we will give the model a coat of flat or satin varnish, depending on personal preference. I like a flat finish, so have used some flat varnish. Give the model twenty-four to forty-eight hours or so to dry, and then you can lightly buff it with some very fine wet-and-dry paper, something like a 3,000 grit. This will serve to remove any slight imperfections in the finish, but shouldn't damage the paintwork.

Area	Brush used	Paint used
Sky under surfaces	Airbrush	Humbrol 90 Sky

10) Transfers and final assembly

The model is pretty much finished at this stage so we can now apply the transfers and add the small exterior detail parts. Paint the propeller, spinner and tyres black, the tips of the prop yellow, and then the various small attachments with the surrounding surface colour.

You can then give the model any weathering you wish to apply, as well as a further flat coat if you wish. This model has received some additional weathering, which will be covered in the weathering section of this book, and has then been mounted onto a flight stand.

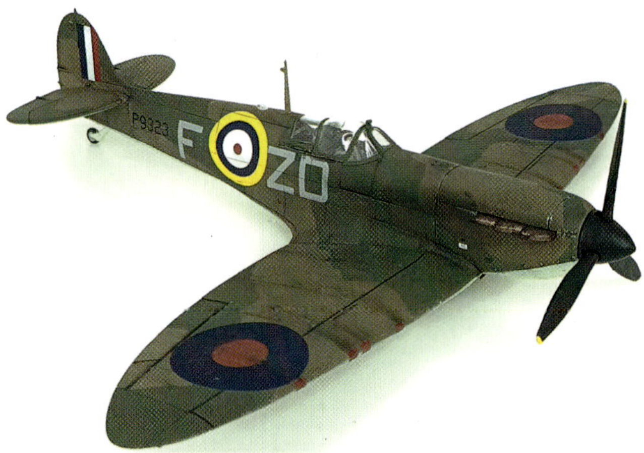

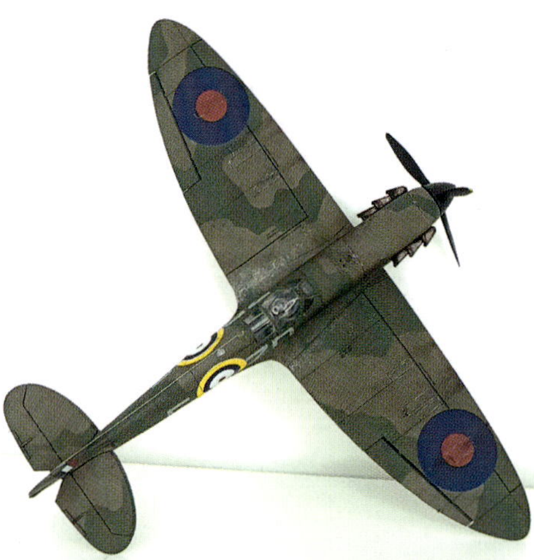

Completed airbrush-painted Spitfire, finished with weathering and transfers.

Above left, above right and left: *This Spitfire represents an aircraft of 66 Squadron flown by Sergeant R.A. Ward which was lost on 8 October 1940. Interestingly, some 66 Squadron aircraft appear to have no standard underside colours as well as red spinners. Both features have been represented on this model.*

Above left and above right: *This Hurricane has had its camouflage airbrushed without masking. While not authentic, it can be used as an example of how this effect could appear on a model. This was achieved by first spraying the outline of the green pattern before filling in the rest of the green areas. Hurricane P3707 served with No. 310 (Czech) Squadron and was lost in a collision with another aircraft of the squadron on 29 October 1940. The pilot of this aircraft was Jaroslav Maly; however, the pilot of the second aircraft, Emil Fechtner, was killed.*

This 605 Squadron Hurricane features standard markings for the period; however, it also features the gas warning patch at the end of the wing. This aircraft would survive the war and still flies to this day.

Defiant L7021 of 264 Squadron has a non-standard black and white spinner as well as a black-painted turret. Masking the spinner required spraying it white and then masking the demarcation line with fine tape. This aircraft was flown by Squadron Leader G.D. Garvin and his gunner Flight Lieutenant R.C.V. Ash. The Defiant was shot down on 28 August 1940. Flight Lieutenant Ash was killed; however, Squadron Leader Garvin survived the war.

3

RAF Night Fighters

In this chapter we will be modelling two Boulton Paul Defiants, the first in 1/72 scale and the second in 1/48 scale. While initially very similar to any other single-seat fighter aircraft model, this one will have some more challenging assembly and a greater requirement for pre-painting and assembly due to the turret system. One will be airbrushed, one will be brush-painted and both will receive different weathering treatments to demonstrate that even a matt black finish can have some visual flare to it.

In 1939 night fighting hadn't particularly advanced beyond that practised twenty-one years earlier in the First World War. Aircraft were largely expected to hunt for enemy aircraft, and ideally find those that were caught in a searchlight and engage them. Airborne Intercept (AI) radar had been in top-secret development in Britain since the 1930s; however, the size and weight of these systems was prohibitive. This was further compounded by the complexity of such systems requiring a dedicated crewman to operate them. This led to the AI sets needing to be fitted to larger, heavier aircraft and the first operational Airborne Intercept-equipped aircraft were modified Bristol Blenheims.

While a very fast and capable aircraft when it first entered service – indeed it had been the first all-metal monoplane combat aircraft to enter RAF service and it outpaced the majority of biplane fighters of the 1930s – the rapid technological development of aircraft in the run-up to the outbreak of war resulted in the Blenheim being outpaced by more modern designs. Nevertheless, the aircraft was modified into a long-range fighter variant with a pack of four Browning machine guns in place of the bomb bay. No. 600 Squadron operating from RAF Manston successfully used Blenheims to down five German bombers on the night of 18 June 1940; however, the lack of speed and comparatively light armament unfortunately meant that this feat was not repeated.

This Defiant is equipped with Airborne Intercept radar. Also worth noting are the presumably silver-painted wheels. **(Kent Battle of Britain Museum Collection)**

The much-maligned Boulton Paul Defiant has drawn a significant amount of unfair criticism over the years. The Defiant was designed to be a bomber destroyer aircraft, operating under the premise that fighters would be unable to escort bombers to their targets. Unlike conventional fighter aircraft with their fuselage and wing-mounted guns, the Defiant's armament consisted of four .303 machine guns in a power-operated turret.

The first sorties for the Defiant took place in May 1940, flying with 264 Squadron. The Defiant proved to be very capable against unescorted bombers as the turret armament meant that fire could be accurately concentrated into a target. No. 264 Squadron also adopted the Lufbery Circle (a defensive air combat tactic), and this decreasing circle would optimise the turret's field of fire while also keeping the aircraft's underside protected.

No. 264 Squadron, along with 141 Squadron, operated the Defiant as a day fighter until 28 August 1940 when mounting losses forced their withdrawal into a night-fighter role, something the Defiant had been intended to fulfil and for which their crews had been trained. As the blitz intensified from October 1940 into the beginning of 1941, the Defiant and the Beaufighter that would supplement and ultimately replace it would continue to see a great deal of use.

While the black night-fighter schemes are technically a little outside the Battle of Britain period, especially for those aircraft used during the blitz, I feel the two periods are inextricably linked so the night fighters belong here alongside their day-fighting colleagues. While I am modelling Defiants, the various painting techniques would apply to any other black-painted aircraft, and could even be combined with other techniques features in this book such as on RAF Bomber Command aircraft.

The two schemes here represent one aircraft earlier in the blitz period serving with 264 Squadron, and the second later in the blitz serving with 151 Squadron. Both aircraft were painted in the standard matt black paint of the period. In January 1941, matt black was to be replaced by RAF Special Night, a type of very dark grey, almost black paint with a distinctly rough matt finish. This weathered heavily and could begin looking pretty worn fairly quickly; however, neither of the subjects here is likely to have been recoated in the new paint. That said, even the matt black finish could start showing wear and tear fairly quickly and exhaust stains are particularly notable on night fighter aircraft.

In 1/48 scale we will be building the Airfix kit to represent Defiant N3313 of 264 Squadron operating in late 1940. The aircraft is associated with several crews in its time with 264 Squadron, including Flying Officer Frederick Desmond Hughes and his gunner Sergeant Fred Gash. Hughes

The real Defiant N3313. The surface is catching the light; however, we can see that there is still some weathering and wear visible on the aircraft. **(Kent Battle of Britain Museum Collection)**

and Gash claimed five German bombers destroyed along with another damaged between August 1940 and April 1941.

For their service Hughes received the DFC and Gash the DFM. Both would survive the war, with Hughes retiring from the RAF in 1974 as an air vice marshal. Fred Gash earned a commission during the war and was released from service in 1945 as a flight lieutenant.

The second build will be an aircraft from 151 Squadron, DZ Z, NZ3328, this time in 1/72 scale. Unfortunately I've not managed to find any crew associated with this aircraft in its role as a combat fighter with 151 Squadron; however, it along with several others from this unit sported a very unusual piece of shark's mouth nose art. Nose art and other non-regulation paint beyond the standard markings were very rare on RAF aircraft, especially fighters.

NZ3328 was taken on strength with 151 Squadron in either November or December 1940 and served with the squadron until April 1942. The aircraft was then taken on as a target tug with 10 Air Gunnery School and was lost in October 1942 when caught in bad weather. Sadly NZ3328 took her pilot with her, a 22-year-old Australian named John Goulter.

We will be building a pair of Airfix Boulton Paul Defiant night fighters, the first of which will be brush-painted in 1/72 scale and the second will be in 1/48 scale. The parts breakdown of both kits is very similar, although the larger model has more detail and complexity. As such a lot of building tips will apply to both models, the 1/72 model will be brush-painted and the 1/48 by airbrush. The 1/72 will be a closed-up model with crew, while the 1/48 model will have the canopies open. As the builds are so similar, we will cover the assembly of both models and then do separate painting guides.

BOULTON PAUL DEFIANT ASSEMBLY

1) Interior assembly

As is standard for an aircraft model, we will start with the interior. While this is fairly standard for any other model aircraft, the addition of the turret does complicate things a little as more sub-assemblies will be

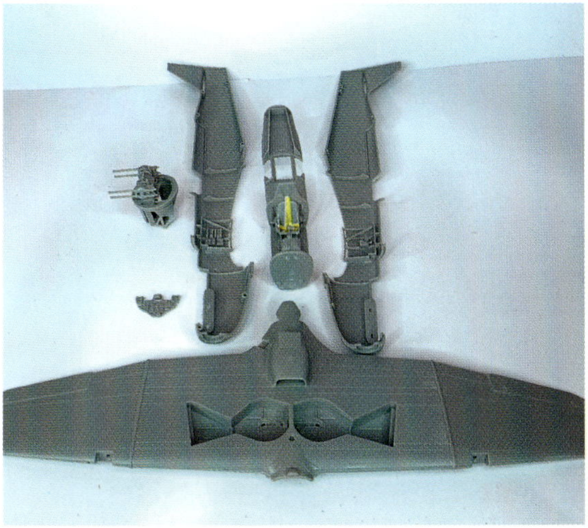

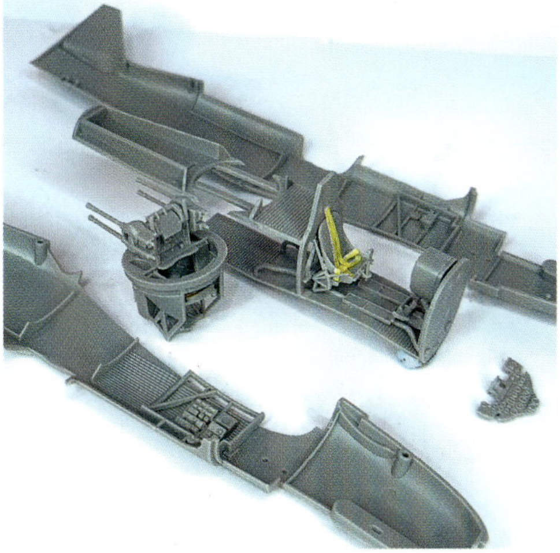

needed and more decisions made regarding assembly of the aircraft due to its moving parts.

Due to the Defiant armament being emplaced in a turret, the airframe had several panels that would be lowered to allow the turret to traverse freely when in combat. These are behind the cockpit canopy, and then the fuselage spine between the turret and the tail.

For both models we will progress through the assembly instructions, adding the detail to the fuselage sides, assembling the seat, floor and bulkheads, and making the control panel. We will also do the turret assembly too, but won't add the glazing to it just yet.

You can decide whether or not to add crew figures, but if you decide not to add them you can add seat belts made from masking tape instead.

2) Interior painting

With the interior parts built, we can paint and prime them as we have done with the Day Fighter guide. These have been painted Interior Green, with black equipment and seat cushion. Any seat belts you add should be painted khaki.

You can also paint the undercarriage wheel well at this time too. Most likely this would be the same colours as the underside of the aircraft; however, you could choose to paint it aluminium at this stage, if you wish, as well as the undercarriage legs and inside of the undercarriage cover doors. You can either brush-paint or spray these parts, whichever you prefer.

Area	Brush used	Paint used
Fuselage sides, seat and floor. Turret interior	Size 2 round	Humbrol 78 Interior Green
Detail parts, seat cushions, instrument panel, machine guns	Size 1 round	Humbrol 33 Matt Black
Undercarriage parts (optional)	Size 1 round	Humbrol 56 Aluminium
Seat belts	Size 1 round	Humbrol 72 Khaki Drill

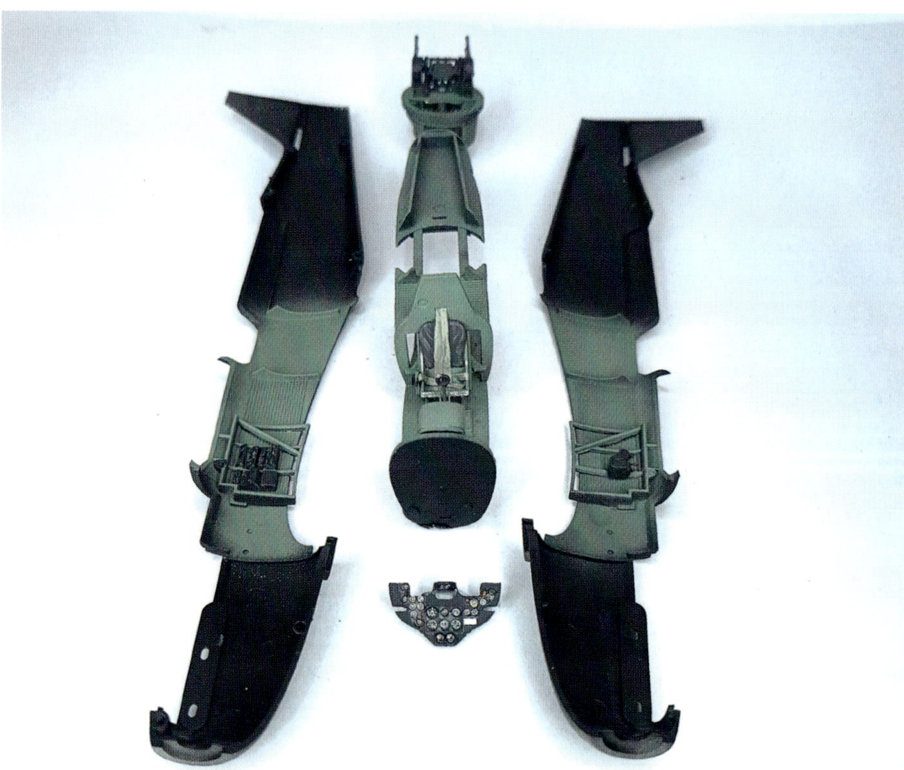

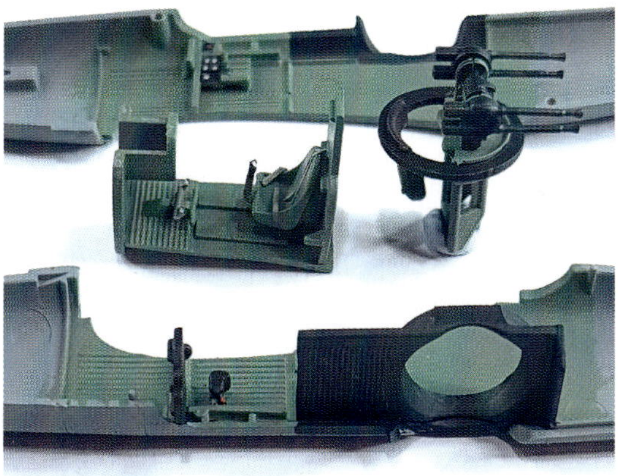

3) Interior weathering

Without wishing to repeat too much, you can refer to the Day Fighters chapter for a few different types of washes you can use. As a third option, here I will present using a clay-based wash product. These function in a fairly similar way to oil washes, although they are water-based so are ideal for those who want to use fewer solvents in their hobby.

Paint the wash into the areas of the model that will naturally catch shadow, leave it to dry for an hour or so and then you can remove it with a damp old brush or cotton bud, using a polishing motion to clean off the excess wash.

Area	Brush used	Paint used
Interior areas	Old size 2	Ultimate Wash Dark Dirt

4) Airframe assembly

Bringing the airframe of the Defiant together can be tricky. The large open area for the cockpit as well as the raising section of the fuselage means that there is a lot of potential for parts to go out of alignment. I'd strongly recommend taking this process slowly. Firstly, fit all the interior parts into place except the gun turret. You can now put that aside until much later in the build.

Then check that the alignment works by fitting both fuselage halves together without glue. You can use masking tape to hold everything together. Once you are happy with the fit, run some thin brush-applied glue such as Humbrol Liquid Poly along the fuselage join. Capillary action should help this flow along all the mating surfaces.

While the fuselage dries you can then build the wings and tail surfaces and add the radiator to the underside of the wings. Leave these to dry too, and then you are free to carry on assembling the aircraft.

The Defiant is a fairly simple model to clean up as most of the seams are hidden along joins on the aircraft. You'll probably only have to clean along the wings and engine cowling, so you shouldn't have too much trouble all being well. Once you are happy with the model's surface, give it wipe down with a damp cloth to get rid of any sanding debris.

With the clean-up complete, we can mask the turret and cockpit canopy. As the 1/48 model is being built with the canopy and turret open, the interior will need additional masking. I've taped over the open ends and added some packing foam into the openings, although you could also simply tape over the openings in the fuselage and turret too.

The model is now ready for a coat of primer and some paint. We will leave off the turret, undercarriage and any other small parts including the exhausts until the model has been built and painted.

5) Prime black

Both of these models which will be painted are due to have a matt black finish, which can be quite dull. However, we will use a few techniques to make this look a little more interesting. To start with both models will

be given a coat of matt black spray, and you can brush-paint or airbrush this on too should you wish.

BRUSH-PAINTING

1) Dark grey surface wear

With the model now painted black, you could go straight on to adding the transfers and small parts and call the model complete. However, you can also paint on some very thinned very dark grey paint and stipple this onto the surface to give the model a worn and used appearance as well as replicating some of the effects of the skinning on the aircraft.

I recommend thinning the paint quite heavily and stippling this onto the surface using a large brush and a make-up blusher brush is ideal for this. Ideally, the paint should be so thin that the first pass of the grey is hard to see. Keep stippling the grey on until you get a level of colour density you are happy with. You can concentrate this effect around the engine and wings where the crew and maintainers would be standing.

Area	Brush used	Paint used
All over the airframe, concentrated in areas of wear	Make-up blusher or chisel-headed	Humbrol 32 Dark Grey

2) Finishing off

Painting a night fighter can be relatively simple so this aircraft has had some light weathering applied, namely some exhaust staining and dust from the crew accessing the aircraft, and is now finished.

Finished, brush-painted Defiant. The shark's mouth nose art was a transfer and applied with significant amounts of Micro Sol/Set.

AIRBRUSH METHOD

1) Dark grey tone variation

Airbrushing this step will give you some very subtle ability to add interest to the model. We will be spraying some dark grey paint into the centre of the panels of the airframe to add some highlights and variation to the model's surface. You can afford to get quite a high level of contrast here as we will be doing more work to the surface shortly.

Spray your dark grey paint into the centre of the panels of the aircraft, gradually achieving a build-up of opacity. Experiment with how your paint flows and dries as all brands are different, and build up a patchwork effect across the surface of the airframe. For further variety you can mix some greens, browns and lighter greys into your dark grey and apply this to some of the aircraft panels too.

The model will currently not be looking especially realistic, so we will spray it with heavily thinned coats of black paint. You will want to mist this paint on, being very careful to prevent the paint from running or streaking. Lightly spray the thinned black paint onto the model, working carefully and slowly and letting one layer dry before applying another. Take your time, and you will have a model with a very interesting subtle surface finish.

Area	Brush used	Paint used
All over the airframe	Airbrush	Humbrol 32 Dark Grey
Selected panels	Airbrush	Humbrol 32 mixed with Humbrol 90 Sky

FINISHING OFF

We can now bring the turret and propeller to the model, add the undercarriage and add the transfers. I like to add a flat coat to the model, and both of these have also received some additional weathering in the form of some panel lining using a darker colour, aluminium chipping along areas of significant wear and finally exhaust staining. An interesting peculiarity of exhaust staining on black-painted aircraft is how it appears as a light grey colour.

With that, the Defiant is finished. These paint techniques translate well to any black-painted aircraft and so could be used on any suitable project you wish.

Above left, above right and overleaf: *The airbrush-painted Defiant. The silver chipping was applied with a sponge.*

4

Luftwaffe Single-Engine Fighters

In this chapter we will be building a pair of Messerschmitt Bf 109s. As with the other builds, we will do a 1/48 scale kit and a 1/72 scale model. German paint schemes can be intimidating, especially without an airbrush, so we will try to break down how to apply these schemes in a simple way. The Bf 109 had an absolutely bewildering array of paint schemes applied between July and October 1940, and it can be tricky to work out the evolution of their camouflage and tactical markings.

The German air force or Luftwaffe had a core of highly experienced pilots as of July 1940, some pilots having flown combat operations in Spain, Poland and the campaigns across Western Europe earlier in the year.

Following the German defeat at the end of the First World War, Germany was prohibited from having a military air arm under the prohibitions of the Treaty of Versailles. Air units of the army and navy were forced to disband in 1920, and their aircraft were either destroyed or handed over to the Allied powers. Given the strategic and tactical importance of military aviation, Germany sought ways around these restrictions. Under the guise of training airline pilots for the national carrier *Deutsche Lufthansa*, personnel were trained under the guise of becoming airline pilots. From 1925, however, a secret training facility was established in the Soviet Union and would continue to operate until 1933. Hundreds of personnel would be trained there, devolving practical skills and knowledge alongside Soviet pilots.

When the Nazis came to power in 1933, however, the façade of compliance with the Treaty of Versailles was dropped. Events moved quickly once the Nazis were established, with Hermann Göring initially being placed in charge of national aviation affairs, then a few months later being made head of the newly-formed Luftwaffe after various aviation and paramilitary organizations were merged.

Glider-flying, a popular hobby in interwar Germany, was not spared the interference of the Nazi state with all private civilian flying organizations being absorbed into the German Airsports Association, and this was further augmented in 1937 by the *Nationalsozialistisches Fliegerkorps* (National Socialist Flyers Corps). These organizations both served the Nazi state by ensuring that avenues of pilot training were open to those interested in developing those skills, and that they could do so in an ideologically approved way. This in turn led to the Luftwaffe having a much higher rate of party membership than either the *Heer* (army) or the *Kriegsmarine* (navy).

Being essentially an entirely new branch of service, the Luftwaffe began developing its doctrine from scratch. Development of aircraft that would ultimately have a military purpose had been under way for some time, notably the Junkers Ju 52, the Focke-Wulf Fw 200 and the Heinkel He 111, and these designs were constrained by the need for secrecy surrounding German rearmament as well as the technology of the time resulting in a preponderance of medium bomber aircraft as the primary offensive force of the Luftwaffe.

This resulted in the Luftwaffe basically being a forced designed to deliver shock attacks in support of ground forces in coordination with ground offensives conducted by the *Heer*. Strategic bombing had been conducted by the Condor Legion, a formation of the German *Heer*, and Luftwaffe personnel assisting fascist forces during the Spanish Civil War. Aircraft more suited to the doctrine were under development as the Second World War began in 1939; however, these would suffer many technical and political issues in entering service and would enter relatively limited service years after the Battle of Britain.

Throughout 1939 and the earlier campaigns of 1940, the German bomber force was largely able to operate in a strategic role given the comparatively limited air arms arranged against them being able to support the ground offensive as well as targeting logistical and strategic infrastructure as necessary. This success gave the Luftwaffe and Göring in particular a skewed and potentially over-inflated sense of the capabilities of the Luftwaffe.

To support the bomber arm, the *Jagdgeschwader* or fighter wings were tasked with establishing air superiority by neutralizing the enemy air forces' ability to resist. This it achieved during the initial campaigns of 1940, destroying the Dutch, Belgian and French air forces as well as driving the Royal Air Force from France. While presented as an overwhelming force, the Luftwaffe did take a bloody nose, losing 36 per cent of its strength to being written off or damaged during the Battle of France. By June these losses were further compounded by the slow supply of new aircraft and pilots in readiness for the Battle of Britain.

As the Luftwaffe caught its breath in June 1940, their attacks on ports and shipping gradually increased throughout June before bringing their full weight to bear against radar stations and ports in July to open their way for a seaborne invasion.

The focus of the Luftwaffe's efforts shifted to attempting to eradicate the RAF presence during August. Pressure was maintained on the radar stations as they proved difficult to take out of action, and a greater emphasis was placed on destroying airfields, particularly those along the coast, with increasingly heavy losses to both sides.

Moving into September, targets were redirected from bombing military bases to bombing civilian centres and Luftwaffe units continued to take heavy casualties. To support their German allies, the Italians sent a small expeditionary force to assist in a series of bombing raids; however, they were of limited success and were poorly equipped. As an aside, much as I would like to have also covered the Italians in this book, the availability of suitable kits is somewhat limited and those kits that are available are of a complexity beyond the scope of this book.

This rapid change in doctrine was reflected in the camouflage patterns and tactical markings applied to German aircraft throughout the period, many applied at a unit level. These changes will be discussed in more detail shortly.

Two types of fighter aircraft were in front-line service with the Luftwaffe during the Battle of Britain period, both produced by Messerschmitt: the single-engine Bf 109 on which we will focus in this chapter and the Bf 110 which we will look at in the next.

The Messerschmitt Bf 109 represented a generational shift when it first flew in 1935. While the Hawker Hurricane was a low-wing monoplane fighter with retractable undercarriage, it was very much an extreme evolution of existing biplane fighters. The Bf 109 stemmed from a specification issued in 1933 by the newly-formed *ReichsLuftfahrtMinisterium* or RLM (the Ministry of Aviation). This specification called for a new high-performance fighter aircraft and oddly, one of the requirements was that the aircraft would be transportable by rail. This led to the aircraft's narrow undercarriage, which would come to make it a punishing aircraft for inexperienced pilots to fly.

One of several competing designs, the Messerschmitt Bf 109 would eventually be chosen as the new primary fighter of the Luftwaffe. First flying in 1935, the new aircraft was sleek, fast and manoeuvrable, becoming the first all-metal fighter with retractable undercarriage to enter operational service, which it did in 1937. The new aircraft would be sent with the Condor Legion to be tested against other modern combat aircraft during the Spanish Civil War, and it proved to be an excellent combat machine, albeit with limited range. The Bf 109 would serve throughout the war and variants would persist in use well after the conflict. Spain, retiring the last of their locally built aircraft in the mid-1960s, gave the Bf 109 a thirty-year service life. It was also the most produced fighter aircraft of all time, although few remain today.

At the outbreak of the Second World War, the Messerschmitt Bf 109 E was the most common combat variant, and although some earlier variants did persist, these were mostly relegated to training and second-line units by the time of the Battle of France. The Bf 109 E was further broken down into several sub-variants and featured fairly significant changes between May and October 1940.

At the start of the Battle of Britain, the E-1 and E-3 variants were the most common. The E-1 was the initial production version and was armed with four 7.92mm MG 17 machine guns. This was half the armament of the Spitfire or Hurricane. The E-2 version carried a cannon firing through the centre of the propeller; however, this had a series of issues and never went into front-line service.

The E-3 saw a further significant increase in the aircraft's capability, the wing machine guns being swapped for 20mm MG FF cannon. These gave a huge increase to the lethality of the aircraft, a hit from one shell being able to bring down most Allied aircraft. The E-3 was further refined into the E-4, which featured a redesigned canopy that would also be fitted to the E-1 and E-3 variants, and improved armour protection for the pilot as well as improvements to the cannon armament. The biggest visual differences between the E-1 and the E-3/4 are the bulges under the wings to accommodate the magazine for the cannon, as well as a flatter windscreen and armour behind the pilot's headrest.

Throughout the course of the Battle of Britain, the short range of the Messerschmitt Bf 109 had really come to affect its performance. Aircraft were unable to spend more than a few minutes in combat over the south coast of Britain, and were struggling to provide acceptable fighter escort and even failing to return to base with alarming frequency due to a lack of fuel. Towards the end of August, the E-7 variant entered service. This was essentially an E-4 with the addition of suitable equipment to carry an external fuel tank, and was also the first major version to be able to carry a bomb load instead of necessary fuel.

This section of Bf 109 demonstrates the RLM 02 paint used both on the interior areas and in the camouflage. Careful examination also shows some RLM 71 Dunkelgrun *with a hard edge to the camouflage pattern. This aircraft was shot down on 14 August 1940 and the pilot Gerhard Kemen survived, although he suffered a broken back. Kemen would be repatriated to Germany and he survived the war.* (Kent Battle of Britain Museum Collection)

Paint schemes would also vary significantly between June and October 1940 for Bf 109 units to reflect the rapidly changing tactical situation.

As Luftwaffe doctrine envisioned their fighter aircraft operating from a position of height and advantage in their role of destroying enemy air forces, the Bf 109 began the war painted in camouflage patterns of dark greens (RLM 70 *Schwartzgrun*, black green and RLM 71 *Dunkelgrun*, dark green) over a light blue (RLM 65 *Hellblau*, light blue) undersurface. However, by the beginning of 1940 this scheme had evolved into one intended to provide optimal camouflage against the sky at altitude. From around August, the RLM 70 *Schwartzgrun* was replaced by a lighter, greenish-grey (RLM 02 *Grau*, grey), and the light blue paint extended up

(Kent Battle of Britain Museum Collection)

Opposite, above and right: *Bf 109 E flown by Franz von Werra crash-landed near Maidstone. This aircraft clearly demonstrates the standard camouflage of Luftwaffe fighters at the beginning of the Battle of Britain. The exhaust staining may be a consequence of the forced landing; however, similar levels of staining appear on still serviceable aircraft as well. Von Werra would be captured, but would eventually manage to escape captivity and return to service with the Luftwaffe, being killed when his aircraft crashed into the sea off the Dutch coast late in 1941. The replica of von Werra's aircraft at the Kent Battle of Britain Museum incorporates original Messerschmitt components, and especially clearly illustrates the Daimler-Benz engine and the casting lines on the exhausts.* **(Kent Battle of Britain Museum Collection)**

the sides of the fuselage and tail so that only a thin strip of camouflage paint was visible in plain view of the aircraft.

While a good scheme for roving fighters, the pattern was also very stark with a high contrast in visibility between the two parts of the pattern, making it quite visible outside a position of advantage.

As the battle progressed, the need for aircraft to escort the bombers became more pressing and placed the fighter units in disadvantageous tactical positions. To reflect their more defensive role greater concealment was required, and so camouflage in the form of mottling would gradually increase on German fighters. This took the form of one or both of the upper surface colours being sprayed onto the fuselage and tail. These were applied at a unit level so they display some fairly extreme variations. Some aircraft appear to have soft oversprays of the lighter green-grey while others have heavy areas of the darker green.

Further still, some aircraft had a series of stripes or hatched lines and still others some soft mottling of both colours. Some aircraft would even

Above left: *Bf 109 Black 14. This aircraft has had a mottle effect applied to the fuselage and tail. It's hard to be certain; however, the aircraft may also have a yellow-painted nose with mottling applied over the yellow paint.* **(Kent Battle of Britain Museum Collection)**

Above right: *Bf 109 of JG 53. These aircraft both appear to have their noses painted yellow, and interestingly have also had heavy oversprays painted possibly with RLM 02* **Grau** *and RLM 71* **Dunkelgrun** *over the wing surfaces. Alternatively RLM 65* **Hellblau** *may have been sprayed over the wing surfaces.* **(Kent Battle of Britain Museum Collection)**

see the painting of the green-grey mottling over the wing surface too in order to further break up the stark lines of their camouflage.

Generally the paint would be sprayed onto the aircraft; however, photographic examples exist showing aircraft that have had the camouflage also applied by paintbrush.

Conversely, as the need for camouflage on aircraft grew, so did the need to distinguish friend from foe. Aircraft would be closing at speeds of hundreds of miles per hour, and especially while fighting among the bombers recognition would prove to be difficult. Relatively early on in the battle, German aircraft began having areas painted in yellow and typically this would be the engine cowlings and rudders, although it could also be the wing and even tail tips depending on the particular unit and the rank or position of the pilot.

Towards the end of the battle, the yellow would be supplemented or replaced by white areas painted onto the aircraft, sometimes quite crudely. These too would be on the cowlings, rudder and wing tips, again depending on the particular squadron.

Bf 109 E7 of JG 53. This aircraft appears to have had the wing guns removed, possibly to save weight and increase range. The aircraft has the red band used to cover up this unit's **Staffel** *badge. The yellow recognition markings appear to have been somewhat hastily applied.* **(Kent Battle of Britain Museum Collection)**

Bf 109 White 9*. This aircraft appears to have a mottled effect painted over both the fuselage sides and possibly the wing upper surfaces as well, although it is difficult to tell. The white recognition marking on the nose also appears to be roughly painted.*
(Kent Battle of Britain Museum Collection)

This wing shows the original RLM 65 paint as well as the RLM 02 **Grau** *used as a primer for the inner areas of the aircraft. Note also the size and position of the cross.* **(Kent Battle of Britain Museum Collection)**

In terms of markings and insignia, the Luftwaffe used a fairly different system to the Royal Air Force. National markings were present on both upper and lower surfaces of the wings, as well as on the fuselage sides. These took the form of a black and white cross, with the ones underneath the wings significantly larger than those on the tops.

Swastikas were painted on the tail, although as the camouflage overpainting became more common these seem to be painted out occasionally so it can be worth trying to find a period photograph of the particular aircraft you are trying to model. It's also worth noting that due to legislation across many European countries, some kits may not include a swastika. These can be ordered in sheets from the likes of Hannants if you should wish to add them.

Other markings take the form of a squadron badge and this would generally be somewhere near the cockpit or on the engine cowling. Numerical or symbol codes were also used. For officers in a staff position, a series of chevrons or geometric shapes, generally black outlined in white, were used. Other aircraft would have either a single or double-digit number painted on the fuselage, generally between the national cross and the cockpit. These would generally be white or yellow, but could sometimes be other colours as well. Personal badges painted below the cockpit or onto the engine cowlings are also used on some aircraft.

From a modelling perspective this gives the builder a wide variety of paint schemes, but must have been a pain logistically.

For the builds we will be working on here, the first will be a 1/48 Bf 109 E-3 from *Jagdgeschwader* 51 flown by Josef 'Pips' Priller. Priller was born in 1915 and was the commander of the 6th *Staffel* (Squadron) of JG 51 during the Battle of Britain. Priller would achieve numerous victories throughout the war and he was often credited, along with his wing man, as being the only Luftwaffe pilot to attack the landing beaches on D-Day in 1944, although this was not the case and other pilots were also active. Priller finished the war with a staff position as Inspector of Day Fighters (West), and would go on to become general manager of the Riegele brewery. In 1961 he died of a heart attack.

Several photos are included of a particular aircraft that appears to have gone through the full evolution of camouflage used during the battle. Early photos demonstrate how the aircraft appeared in the standard light blue and camouflaged upper fuselage, whereas pictures towards the end of the battle show yellow identification markings and lots of heavy overspraying of camouflage mottling, including over the wings.

This model will be airbrushed, and will be a good demonstration of how to apply the various camouflage schemes to a Bf 109 using a freehand technique.

Bf 109 White 5, the subject of the 1/72 Airfix Bf 109 kit. The photo here demonstrates the heavy mottling effect applied to the aircraft. **(Kent Battle of Britain Museum Collection)**

The second build we will be making is a 1/72 scale Bf 109 E-4, as flown by *Unteroffizier* Hans-Georg Schulte of 7 *Staffel*, JG 53. Much like Priller's aircraft, this one also shows various stages of painting through the course of the battle and has also ended up with both heavy mottling and some pretty rough-looking white recognition markings.

Hans-Georg Schulte had served with JG 53 during the Battle of France, and had proven to be a successful pilot with numerous victories to his name. On 6 September 1940, however, Schulte was forced to make a crash-landing near Manston in Kent, where he was captured and spent the rest of the conflict as a prisoner of war. Schulte's aircraft, being relatively intact, was used as a propaganda piece and was sent on to be displayed around the United Kingdom to raise funds for the war effort.

The aircraft of JG 53 had a fairly unique appearance owing to their commanding officer Major Hans-Jürgen von Cramon-Taubadel being married to a Jewish woman. Upon being made aware of this fact, Göring ordered JG 53 to cover their unit, the *Pik As* ('Ace of Spades'), emblem with a red band as a mark of shame around the engine cowlings of their aircraft. As a sign of protest, JG 53 then painted out the swastika from their aircraft.

The aircraft being flown by Schulte appears to have the red band and no swastika. The red band has been painted over with white recognition markings, although the paint appears to have been hastily applied so some traces of the red remain visible.

Camouflage seems to consist of the standard Luftwaffe fighter colours, with a heavy mottling of dark green applied over most of the fuselage. We will be using a brush to paint this particular model to demonstrate techniques to apply the heavy mottle effect with thin glazes of paint.

The two Messerschmitt Bf 109s we will be building here are again going to feature one brush-painted and one airbrushed model. These will have rather more complex painting patterns as we will be applying mottling as well as a mix of hard- and soft-edged camouflage patterns. These are difficult schemes to pull off even for experienced modellers, so I'd recommend getting some plasticard and practising these techniques on it before you commit to painting the model itself.

AIRFIX 1/72 MESSERSCHMITT BF 109

Here we will be building another classic kit, the opposition to the Airfix 1/72 Spitfire. This is a slightly more complex kit than the Spitfire and features the option for an open engine bay, open canopy and dropped flaps. As we'll be modelling this aircraft in flight, a little more care will be needed in lining everything up on the model to ensure it all fits together correctly.

1) Initial assembly

The kit's instructions call for you to assemble the propeller and cockpit in the first few stages of the instructions. We will do so here, although with an optional alteration.

As this example is to be modelled in flight, one way that it can be made to appear more realistic is to represent the spinning effect of the propellers. To do this, we will trim off the propeller blade down to the hub before attaching the spinner assembly. Once the model is completed, we will add some clear plastic sheet cut to represent spinning props. For clarity, this will be covered in more detail later in the book.

To build the cockpit, assemble the floor, seat, stick, rudder pedals (these may require some trimming to be able to accommodate the pilot)

and the pilot himself. We are adding the pilot now as the whole kit sub-assembly is easily reachable by brush and it will save excessive handling of the pilot figure later in the build.

Leave the control panel separate at this stage as it is to be painted a different colour. I'd also suggest cleaning up the fuselage parts, and checking that the cockpit fits well as we will be painting the fuselage sides as well in the next stage.

2) Interior painting

The colours for the interior of German aircraft are a bit of a minefield. Broadly speaking, up until November 1941 they were painted a greenish-grey colour before switching to a very dark grey.

However, some aircraft, depending on type and where they were manufactured, appeared to have had the dark grey in part or all of their cockpits. For the builds featured here, we will stick to the officially prescribed colours and paint all the interior in RLM 02 *Grau*. This colour is also suitable for the wheel wells, inner gear bay doors and undercarriage legs.

With the grey dried, we can also pick out the side wall details on the fuselage as well as the instrument panel and for these we will use black-grey. The lower part of the gun sight also needs picking out in this colour so we will do that now.

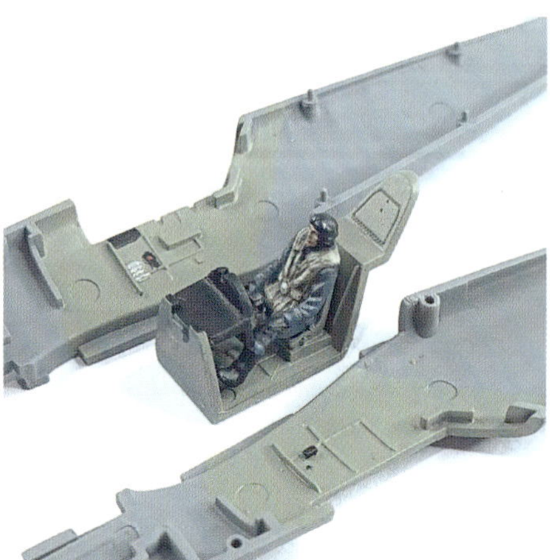

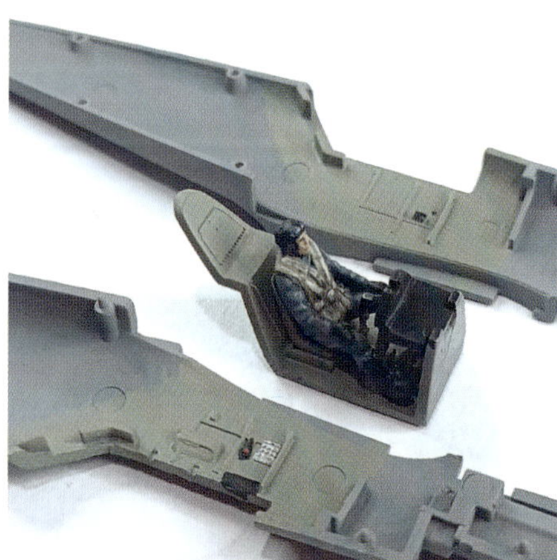

Area	Brush used	Paint used
Interior areas	Size 2 round	Humbrol 240 RLM 02 *Grau*
Detail parts and instrument panel	Size 1 round	Humbrol 32 Dark Grey

3) Finishing the interior

We will add the instrument panel decal, paint the pilot and add a thin wash to the aircraft's interior to pick out the details. You could use a dark grey or dark brown, but we will use a very dark green instead. Mix a little paint with some water and paint this over RLM 02 surfaces of the model, lifting the paint where it starts to pool but allowing it to remain in the recesses.

Details on painting the pilot will be covered in the figure-painting section of this book.

Area	Brush used	Paint used
Interior areas	Size 2 round	Humbrol 242 RLM 71 *Dunkelgrun*

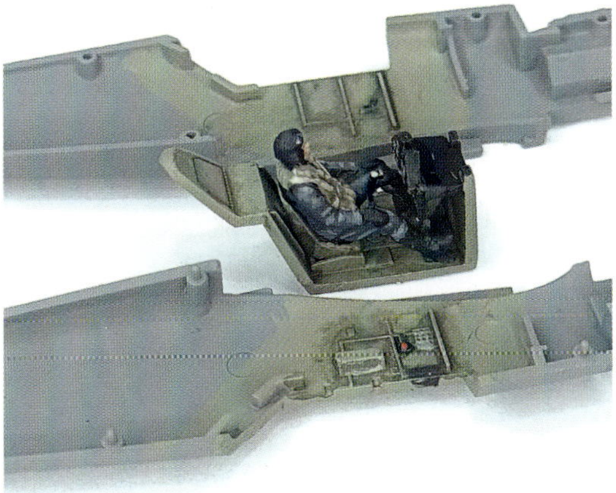

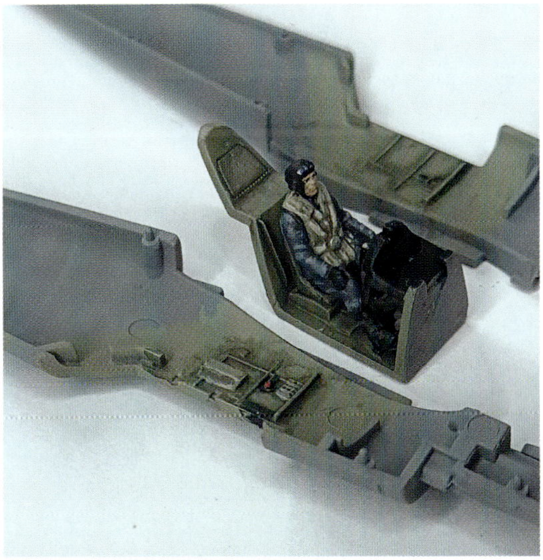

4) Building the aircraft

We will now follow the instructions, bringing the aircraft together. We can add the propeller spinner too as it will be the same colour as the engine cowling and doesn't have any prop blades we can break off.

One peculiarity of the Bf 109 family was the seam along the fuselage. This makes joining the fuselage a little more complex as you need to exercise a little more care. The best way to join the halves is to hold or tape together the fuselage, and then use a thin liquid cement such as Humbrol Liquid Poly or Tamiya Extra Thin to flow along the joint. Be careful not to apply too much pressure to this as it can cause the plastic to melt together and squeeze out of the join. Normally this would be useful for filling the gaps, but in this instance we want to preserve it.

Bringing the wings and tail assembly to the model, we will add the bracing struts to the tail of the aircraft but leave off the tail wheel and other small, delicate parts. As this model is being built in the flying configuration we will add the closed wheel bay doors, although if you are making the model on the ground, leave off the undercarriage until the model is painted. We will also leave the exhausts until after the model is painted.

This particular kit, and most other modern-tooled Bf 109s, has parts for dropped flaps on the model, and these are secured at the correct angle via tabs. To model the aircraft in flight, simply trim these tabs off

as indicated in the instructions and then add them so that they are flush with the wing.

To fit the canopy, start by fitting the windscreen, then the aft panel and finally the centrepiece. We will use some PVA or specific modelling canopy glue to fit the canopy as even with dry fitting it will allow us to manoeuvre the parts into position to get a good fit. You can either mask the parts before or after you fit them to the model. My preference, though, is to mask before fitting as it means you are handling the parts less once they are actually on the model.

Leave the model to fully dry, and then you can paint the canopy black before giving the model a coat of primer. I'd recommend a grey primer for this particular scheme.

5) Initial painting

We'll be painting this model in much the same way that the real aircraft appears to have been painted. As such, we'll be giving it the light blue fuselage sides and two-tone camouflage on the wings and fuselage before adding the dark mottling and overspray seen on the aircraft before adding the specific recognition markings.

To begin with we'll be painting the undersides of the aircraft with RLM 65 Light Blue. The reasons for this are twofold. Firstly, it is the colour found on the majority of the aircraft, especially before it received the camouflage mottling, and secondly it is much easier to paint a lighter

colour over the grey than if we were trying to cover up any of the dark green or grey once the camouflage is applied.

Thin the paint with water and using a medium to large brush apply the blue to the model. Work carefully, not allowing the paint to build up or pool. As this is such a light colour, you will probably need to use multiple coats to get a decent opaque coverage. It's much better to add too thin a layer of paint than one too thick. Once you have built up a solid blue colour, leave the model to dry overnight as we will be applying masking tape in the next step.

Area	Brush used	Paint used
Lower areas and fuselage sides	Size 4 round	Humbrol 65 Aircraft Blue

6) RLM 02 Grey camouflage

Before we start applying the camouflage, we will be masking off the areas of the model that are going to remain light blue. While the wing to fuselage joints don't necessarily need masking, you can use some tape to mask the join if you wish. More important is the demarcation line between the light blue on the fuselage and the camouflage colours. We'll use some 4mm masking tape to run a line of tape along the side of the fuselage, running from the level of the base of the canopy to the base of the tail. I'd also suggest adding some tape along the trailing and leading

edges of the wings as it's very easy to have paint leak or run over the edges if you aren't careful.

With the model masked up, we will now add some RLM 02 *Grau* over the upper surface of the model. Be careful when painting next to the masked areas that the paint doesn't leak or run under the tape. Again, you may need a couple of coats to get an opaque finish.

Area	Brush used	Paint used
Lower areas and fuselage sides	Size 4 round	Humbrol 240 RLM 02 *Grau*

7) RLM 71 *Dunkelgrun*

With the grey in place, we can now add the dark green disruptive pattern. You can mask this with tape; however, I prefer to do this by eye and freehand the pattern. The standard day fighter pattern was a set pattern repeated across the majority of Bf 109s and is well documented, with most kits showing this pattern in their instructions. The trick to painting original camouflage patterns is to identify where the shapes of the pattern form in relation to the panels and details on the aircraft.

Take your time in applying the pattern, and remember that any mistakes can easily be rectified. I suggest painting in the outline of the dark green areas first before blocking in the rest of the colour. This will ensure that you have a neat, sharp outline.

This would also be a good way to represent an aircraft in the standard fighters' colours during the early part of the Battle of Britain.

Area	Brush used	Paint used
Lower areas and fuselage sides	Size 2 round	Humbrol 242 RLM 71 *Dunkelgrun*

8) Grey mottling

With the camouflage done, we will now remove the masking tape from the fuselage. Sometimes the paint can build up into a ridge where it meets the tapes, but this is easily sanded away with some 2,000 grit wet-and-dry paper. You can also neaten up any paint that has flowed under the masks at this stage too.

Mottling is a difficult but impressive-looking camouflage. The aircraft we are representing has a heavy overspray of RLM 71 *Dunkelgrun*; however, from photos this appears to have been sprayed over some RLM 02 *Grau*.

First of all we will use a large, soft brush to stipple on layers of the grey. Thin the paint quite heavily and apply this all along the sides of the aircraft as well as the tail. Leave this to dry, and then add another layer. Repeat this until you have a rough, grey finish on the sides of the aircraft.

Area	Brush used	Paint used
Lower areas, fuselage sides	Size 4 round	Humbrol 240 RLM 02 *Grau*

9) Dark green mottling

This aircraft had a significant area of dark green camouflage on its upper surface. The shape this covers is quite distinctive, so we will firstly paint a very light layer of dark green onto the model over the areas that require covering, and then using the same stippling motion build up the opacity of the colour over several successive layers. Don't forget to leave an RLM 02 *Grau* square on the tail where the swastika was painted out.

The particular aircraft I'm modelling also featured a mottling on the wings as well, and I've repeated the dark green mottling there.

Area	Brush used	Paint used
Lower areas and fuselage sides	Size 2 round	Humbrol 242 RLM 71 *Dunkelgrun*

10) Optional red band

This particular aircraft from JG 53 had a red band painted on the nose during part of its service life, and while it is largely obscured by the later white recognition marking on the cowling there is still a subtle trace of it. You could go straight to painting the white cowling; however, we will be adding a representation of the red band to this model.

To get some neat edges, we will mask off a band 3.5mm wide before painting it with red paint. The paint doesn't need to be thinned too much for this, just enough so that it flows from the brush. You don't want the paint to be too thin though, otherwise it will bleed under the tape.

Area	Brush used	Paint used
Lower areas and fuselage sides	Size 2 round	Humbrol 60 Scarlet

11) White cowling and spinner

We will now finish the painting of the aircraft by masking off the engine cowling and painting it white. From photos this paint appears to be very rough, so we will use the stippling technique we used on the mottling to build up the opacity of the white.

Start off by applying a thin overall layer of white. Let this dry, and then repeat with multiple successive layers to get a patchy white finish on the aircraft. With that we can remove the masking, add the transfers and the small parts, finishing off the model.

Area	Brush used	Paint used
Lower areas and fuselage sides	Size 4 round	Humbrol 34 White

12) Finishing off

The finished model has now had transfers and weathering applied, as well as a few extra steps to add the model to a flight stand which will be covered in a later chapter.

AIRFIX 1/48 MESSERSCHMITT BF 109

This build will showcase building a model with dropped flaps and slats and an open canopy, as well as airbrushing complex mottling camouflage. This build will feature far more sub-assemblies than our previous models as it will make life much easier when it comes to painting. With regard to the complexity of the mottling, we will be doing a fine series of mottles so I strongly suggest experimenting with how you thin your paint and which air pressure you use to spray to get the finest lines you can.

It's also worth mentioning that this model is a slight departure from the kit-supplied painting instructions and represents the same aircraft from earlier on in the Battle of Britain.

1) Initial construction

We'll start by building the model into several sub-assemblies. As we're going to be airbrushing the majority of this model, we can get away with building quite significant parts of it now. Take a moment to go through the instructions, and familiarize yourself with how the various parts go together and attach to the aircraft itself. There are a few parts that will also need prepping and drilling out so that you can add parts later in the build so keep an eye out for those. While I am specifically building the Airfix kit, these techniques and tips also apply to any kit on which you are working.

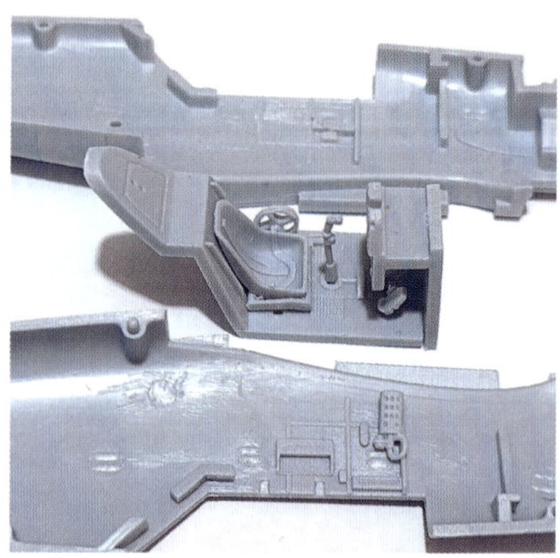

We will begin by building the following areas of the kit: the cockpit tub, the seat and the control panel as one unit. Add the detail parts to the fuselage sides, but do not join the fuselage halves together.

It's also worth preparing the major wing parts and undercarriage so that they can all be painted at the same time. It's also worth building the radiators as these can be painted before being added to the aircraft as well.

2) Internal painting

We'll start by priming these parts with a black spray, and once this is dry we will start by spraying some RLM 02 *Grau* over the interior. Areas to be painted are all of the cockpit components, the wheel wells and the radiator insides. When applying the grey, mist on a light coat, let it dry to the touch and then start building up the opacity of the colour. We are aiming to get a bit of a tonal range with the darkest tones in the recesses.

With the grey dry, we can pick out the relevant details in black, namely the instrument panel and various switches around the interior as well as the radiator faces. Once this is dry, we can give the seat a dry brush of aluminium to simulate chipped paint if you wish. Finally, pick out the seatbelts and cuff at the base of the control column with khaki. Pick out the buckles on the belts in silver.

As we're working on the rest of the undercarriage parts, we may as well paint the wheels too. We'll paint the tyres dark grey and the hubs in black. If you have it, use gloss black for the wheel hubs. If you wish to use an instrument panel decal, now is a good time to add it.

Area	Brush used	Paint used
Cockpit and wheel well area, undercarriage components and radiator internals	Airbrush	Humbrol 240 RLM 02 *Grau*
Detail areas	Size 2 round	Humbrol 33 Matt Black

Area	Brush used	Paint used
Chipping on seat, seat buckles and parts of undercarriage legs	Flat brush for dry brushing Size 1 round for details	Humbrol 56 Aluminium
Seat belts and control column cuff	Size 1 round	Humbrol 26 Khaki
Wheels	Size 2 round	Humbrol 32 Dark Grey for tyres Humbrol 21 for hubs

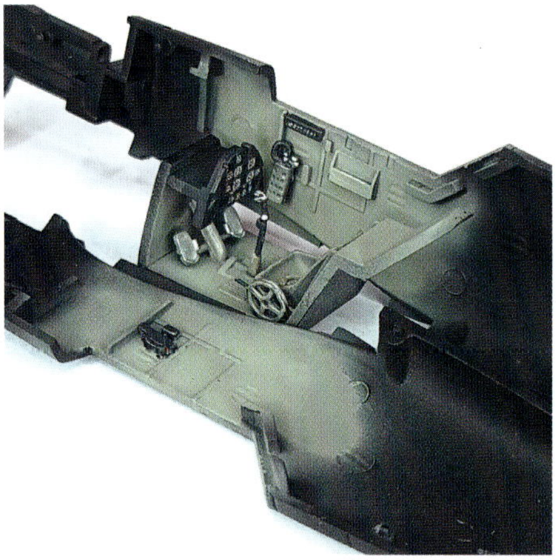

3) Optional interior finishing

Before closing the model up, we will add a pin wash of a dark brown paint. Any homemade or pre-mixed wash is fine for this, and I've used some raw umber oil paint mixed into a wash as it's my personal preference; however, you can use whichever method you prefer. Apply the wash, then clean it up so that the wash remains confined to the details and recesses, highlighting the detail of the area.

Area	Brush used	Paint used
Cockpit and wheel well area, undercarriage components and radiator internals	Old size 2 brush	Winsor & Newton Raw Umber

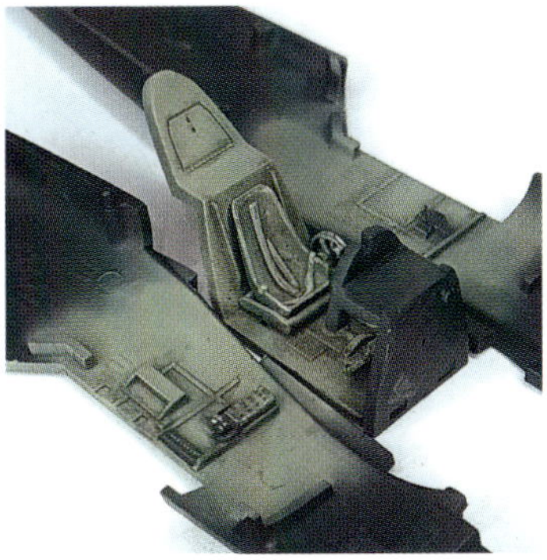

4) Aircraft assembly

Now that the interior and sub-assemblies are painted, we can start building the full airframe of the aircraft. I've decided to build the model with the flaps and slats down so will be leaving these off for the initial assembly and painting. We will prepare the parts though, and check that they fit well onto the model. This will allow us to adjust any fit issues before we need to start handling a painted model.

As with the 1/72 scale build, be mindful of the seam line along the spine of the fuselage. You can always rescribe it if you need to, but a bit of careful assembly can save you a job.

Due to the somewhat complex nature of this aircraft's paint scheme, I've cleaned up and test-fitted the parts of the propeller but have left them off the model. I've also left off the aircraft's rudder as this will save masking it later. I'll leave off the small parts and canopy until the model is

painted, but add the tail struts again. Any small parts that we've taken off the sprue to clean up or are a sub-assembly we will keep in a safe, sealed container until they are painted and ready to add to the model.

With the airframe complete, we can finish prepping and filling the areas that need it and then prime the model ready for painting. I'll be priming the Bf 109 in grey to check for any defects before spraying the model black as a base from which to paint once I am happy with the surface.

5) Yellow areas

Significant areas on this aircraft were painted with yellow recognition markings. Yellow can be a difficult colour with which to get coverage so can work better over a white base. If you're having trouble with coverage, try spraying the area white first.

Here I've sprayed the yellow over the grey primer, but have built up the opacity of the colour by misting on several light coats to establish a base before filling in the tone in the centre of the panels. Keep building up light coats until you are happy with the colour.

Once this is painted, leave the model to dry at least overnight before masking off the yellow areas. I've used some thin strips of tape to mask the areas where the yellow meets the camouflage before using thicker tape to cover the rest of the yellow areas.

Area	Brush used	Paint used
Nose and rudder	Airbrush	Humbrol 24 Yellow

6) Spray the blue

We will now spray the light blue onto the model. We're going to spray this to build up a smart opaque finish, misting on layers to begin with before filling in individual panels to get a strong opaque finish. Don't forget to paint the underside of the flaps and the exterior of the wheel well doors. Once you are satisfied with the finish of the blue, again leave it to dry overnight and we can mask off the model ready for applying the camouflage.

Area	Brush used	Paint used
Fuselage and tail, underside of wings, underside of flaps and exterior of undercarriage doors	Airbrush	Humbrol 65 Aircraft Blue

7) Spray the RLM 02 *Grau*

We're going to spray the RLM 02 *Grau* on the model first. While you could switch this and the *Dunkelgrau* around, with the dropped slats we would need to paint their housing in RLM 02 anyway so it's a little easier to spray these at the same time as the rest of the aircraft's upper surfaces. Once the *Grau* is dry we can mask off the slat housing.

I want a sharp edge to the camouflage so will use masking tape to mask out the camouflage pattern. However, if you are modelling an aircraft with a softer pattern, you could use masking putty or cut templates from card.

Area	Brush used	Paint used
Wings, tail, fuselage, tops of flaps, slats and slat housing	Airbrush	Humbrol 240 RLM 02 *Grau*

8) Paint the RLM 71 *Dunkelgrun*

Now we're in a position to add the dark green overspray of the camouflage onto the aircraft. Simply spray the dark green into the masked areas, being careful to spray close to the masked areas to ensure that paint

does not bleed or flow under the tape. This would also be how we would paint an aircraft from the early part of the Battle of Britain.

Area	Brush used	Paint used
Camouflage pattern areas	Airbrush	Humbrol 242 RLM 71 *Dunkelgrun*

9) RLM 02 *Grau* mottling

We'll now peel off the camouflage from the fuselage and tail surface. You may need to use a brush to neaten up any paint that's run under the tape. Hopefully you won't need to, but it's important to know how to rectify any damage to paint or any mistakes.

To begin the mottling, we will mix a thin layer of RLM 02 *Grau*. Practise spraying away from the model, and then lightly spray a sequence of squiggles and blobs onto the fuselage. You'll also want to carry this mottling up along the demarcation line between the camouflage and the blue as this appears to have been partially overpainted on the real aircraft.

Area	Brush used	Paint used
Fuselage sides	Airbrush	Humbrol 240 RLM 02 *Grau*

10) RLM 71 *Dunkelgrun* mottling

To finish the camouflage the aircraft needs a heavy overspraying of dark green mottling. This is most heavily concentrated around the cockpit and then becomes a looser pattern towards the tail. With that the camouflage is done. We can peel off the remaining masking tape and give the aircraft a coat of flat or satin varnish.

Area	Brush used	Paint used
Fuselage sides and rudder	Airbrush	Humbrol 242 RLM 71 *Dunkelgrun*

11) Completion

The aircraft is now mostly painted so we can add the transfers and give the model another flat or satin coat as well as any weathering. Now we can bring together all the sub-assemblies. I'd suggest saving the canopy as the very last part to be added to the model as it protrudes awkwardly from the fuselage so it can be broken or knocked off too easily.

Above left and above right: *This aircraft represents an example from early in the battle, with pale blue fuselage sides and hard-edged RLM 02 and RLM 71 camouflage. The aircraft modelled here was flown by the famous ace Adolf Galland. Galland would serve throughout the war, completing his service with the rank of general.*

Above left and above right: *Bf 109 of JG 52, White 2. The aircraft represented here is very representative of the markings used on Bf 109s during the battle with yellow recognition markings on the nose and tail, although the large cat picture is unusual. This aircraft was damaged in combat and made a forced landing at RAF Detling. The pilot Erich Mummert would spend the rest of the war as a PoW.*

Above left and above right: *Bf 109 E-7, White 12 of JG 53. The aircraft has the later more aerodynamic nose spinner and a heavy camouflage mottle. More areas of yellow recognition markings have been applied to the aircraft and the tail swastika has also been painted out at some stage. This aircraft crash-landed in Strood in Kent. It was flown by Ernst Poschenrieder, who would spend the remainder of the war as a PoW. Surprisingly the crash site was visited by a film crew and footage of it can be found on YouTube.*

5

Luftwaffe Heavy Fighters

Development of the Messerschmitt Bf 110 began in the mid-1930s following an RLM-issued specification for a fighter-bomber aircraft with cannon armament and internal bomb bay. Junkers and Arado issued submissions; however, it was the Messerschmitt design that proved to be sleeker, faster and better armed, and although it eschewed the internal bomb bay, it would have the capacity to carry a bomb load in later versions.

First flying in 1936, the Bf 110 would begin entering squadron service in 1938. The Luftwaffe's new fighter was unlike any other aircraft then in service. The Bf 110 was an aerodynamically very clean aircraft with a two- or sometimes three-man crew, with a very heavy armament of two cannon and four forward-firing machine guns in the nose as well as a single rearward-firing machine gun. The aircraft had a respectable speed and very long range. It became something of a focus for propaganda and was a favourite of Hermann Göring.

Entering service too late to see service during the Spanish Civil War, the Messerschmitt Bf 110 would serve during the Polish, Norwegian and Low Countries campaigns, as well as during the Battle of France. The Bf 110 was used in an air superiority role during these campaigns, where it proved very capable against the aircraft of those air forces.

The Bf 110 also proved itself during this early period of the war as a bomber destroyer, engaging the first of the air raids conducted by the Royal Air Force where its heavy armament proved well suited to the task. While not as fast as most single-engine fighters, the aircraft was fast enough to catch and destroy bombers. However, this so far excellent track record was to be abruptly challenged during the Battle of Britain.

While the Bf 109 was an excellent fighter, it did not have the range to comprehensively escort the bombers. Luftwaffe doctrine at the start of the battle called for the escorts to fly slowly and close to their charges. This robbed the escorting fighters of height, speed and positioning advantages, as well as causing the Bf 109s to burn precious fuel in the protracted formatting process.

With its good range, the Bf 110 would seem to have been a good choice as an escort for the bomber squadrons; however, the aircraft was intended to use its speed to engage from a position of advantage and then reposition for another attack run. Being shackled to slow-flying bombers, the Bf 110's slow acceleration and poor manoeuvrability led to it suffering very heavy losses. Between 15 and 17 August 1940, for example, more than fifty Bf 110s were shot down. Indeed, of the 237 Bf 110s available at the start of July, almost all of these were no longer operational by the end of October 1940. While these losses were appalling, the Bf 110 would still prove to be effective against the Spitfires and Hurricanes when able to operate freely. The aircraft would also find its new niche as a ground-attack aircraft, flying with *Erprobungsgruppe* (test wing) 210. This wing's aircraft were equipped with a respectable bomb load and were tasked with attacking radar stations and airfields along the south coast, causing significant damage to Ventnor radar station on 13 August 1940.

Erprobungsgruppe 210 also took part in a low-level raid on RAF Hawkinge on 15 August, contributing to significant damage caused to the airfield as well as civilian and RAF personnel deaths. Despite this, the damage was swiftly patched up and the airfield remained operational.

The Messerschmitt Bf 110 would go on to serve successfully as a heavy fighter, operating in ground-attack roles, as a bomber destroyer and most successfully as a night fighter, and would remain in front-line service until the end of the war.

From 1939 Luftwaffe aircraft were painted in a two-tone green splinter camouflage pattern, the official paint codes being RLM 70 *Schwartzgrun* (black green) and RLM 71 *Dunkelgrun* (dark green) over RLM 65 *Hellblau* (light blue) under-surfaces. While the Messerschmitt Bf 109 transitioned to the lighter more disruptive pattern at the beginning of 1940 and gradually evolved to have mottling throughout the course of the summer, the Bf 110 retained the darker pattern until August 1940.

A good portrait image of a ZG 76 Bf 110. This aircraft is particularly clean-looking and gives a good view of a shark's mouth design. (Kent Battle of Britain Museum Collection)

It's also worth noting that the two-tone camouflage pattern was used on pretty much every type of bomber, trainer, transport and even rescue aircraft used by the Luftwaffe. As such, while not covered in this book, you could use the techniques here for almost any of the modelling projects of this period.

This pattern was intended to conceal the aircraft against the ground on the assumption that attacking fighters would be closing from above, thus requiring the bomber to be harder to spot over land. As the Messerschmitt Bf 110 was largely operating alongside the bombers as an escort, it was deemed necessary for it to utilize the same camouflage. However, as the battle progressed and the Bf 110 was used in a tactically more aggressive way, they began to be repainted. The RLM 70 black green was repainted, sometimes roughly, with RLM 02 grey. Along

This section of a Junkers Ju 88 tail has a large area of very well preserved RLM 70 Schwartzgrun. *When placed next to the black of the swastika it shows just how dark a shade this paint was.* (Kent Battle of Britain Museum Collection)

the fuselage sides and vertical tail grey or RLM 65 light blue would also be applied, over which a mottled pattern was then added using either a spray gun or a brush.

Here we will be building two 1/72 Airfix kits of the Messerschmitt Bf 110. The first will be an aircraft in the two-tone green hard-edged camouflage. This aircraft served with II *Staffel Zerstörergeschwader* 76. I've not been able to find anything about the crew of this particular aircraft; however, this machine is also probably the subject of the most famous photograph of the Bf 110 during the Battle of Britain, flying over the English Channel with a coastal town below.

Zerstörergeschwader 76 was a highly-experienced formation by the time of the Battle of Britain, having fought in all the war's air campaigns until that point, and had a great deal of success against their opposition. Their fate during the Battle of Britain would largely mirror that of the Messerschmitt Bf 110, however, and they would incur huge losses throughout the course of the battle, losing twelve aircraft on 15 August alone.

Interestingly from a modelling perspective, their aircraft wore a very distinctive shark's mouth painted on the nose of their aircraft and were in fact the first formation to do so in the Second World War.

***A third ZG 76 aircraft, this time with the entire nose having a rough coat of white paint. The paint appears to have significantly streaked and run during its application. This aircraft was shot down on 11 September 1940 and was crewed by* Feldwebel *Brinkmann and* Unteroffizier *Grüschow. Both survived the crash-landing to become prisoners of war.* (Kent Battle of Britain Museum Collection)**

This ZG 76 Bf 110 has had a white recognition panel applied to its nose. Careful examination of the image shows a relatively rough application of the white paint as well as some subtle weathering on the airframe. (Kent Battle of Britain Museum Collection)

This image of a 1.ZG 26 Bf 110 gives a good clear view of the Staffel *badge, as well as showing a nice detail on the radio antenna mast. This photo probably dates to the Battle of France.* (Kent Battle of Britain Museum Collection)

This aircraft will be painted with an airbrush to demonstrate masking a hard-edged splinter type camouflage pattern.

The second build will be of an aircraft belonging to I *Gruppe Zerstörergeschwader* 26. This aircraft was crewed by *Oberleutnant* Rüdiger Proske and his gunner *Unteroffizier* H. Moebius.

I've not been able to find much information about Moebius. However, Proske took over as adjutant of I *Gruppe*, inheriting his predecessor's aircraft which had been marked with a painting of a pencil to signify his disdain for the paperwork side of the position. On 18 August 1940 Proske and Moebius were shot down, probably by Squadron Leader A.R.D. MacDonell of 64 Squadron, crash-landing near Lydd on the Kent coast. They would spend the rest of the war as PoWs.

Proske and Moebius' aircraft wears the later mottled camouflage with the RLM 70 Black Green being replaced by RLM 02 Grey, and will be a good contrast to the ZG 76 aircraft. We will be brush-painting this model to demonstrate how to paint the lighter mottle effects with a brush.

We're going to be building a pair of 1/72 Airfix Bf 110C kits here, including a set of aftermarket transfers from AIMS (Stab Bf 110s). There is a huge variety of transfers available on the aftermarket, and these can really open up the range of subjects available to you, especially when there is a kit of a subject that you particularly enjoy building.

As both kits are essentially the same, I'll be keeping the assembly sequences the same for both brush and airbrush builds before splitting to differentiate between brush and airbrush. This guide especially shows up some of the specifics of painting German bomber and ground-attack aircraft so could translate towards painting these as well.

1) Initial assembly

As with most aircraft kits, we'll start by building the internal parts. We'll get all the cockpit component parts put together: the seats, the floor and the cannon magazines. We'll also add the undercarriage bays to the wings. You can decide at this point if you want to add crew figures. I've decided against it, and added seat belts made from masking tape instead.

 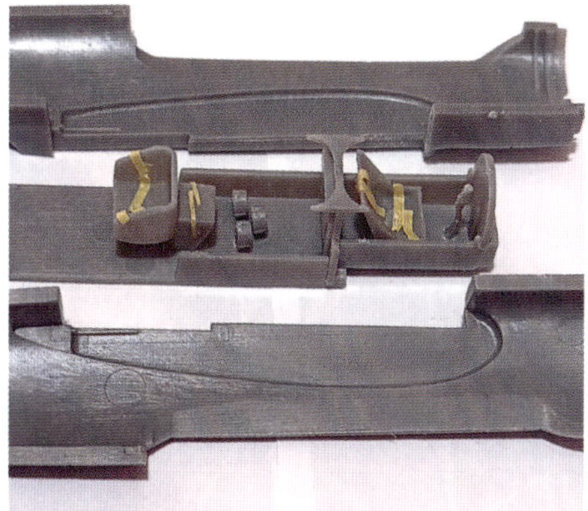

We can also clean up and paint the parts for the undercarriage. We won't fit them until the model is painted, but as we're using the same colours for the other interior parts, it makes sense to prepare and paint them now.

2) Interior painting

To paint the interior, you can prime the parts. If you are airbrushing, I'd suggest using black as a base coat. If you are brush-painting, you can either clean the parts in some washing-up liquid or give them a coat of primer. I'd suggest using a grey if you're brush-painting. This will make paint coverage easier.

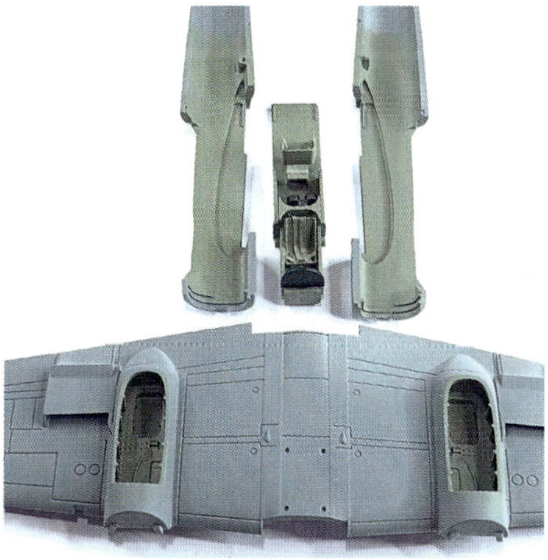 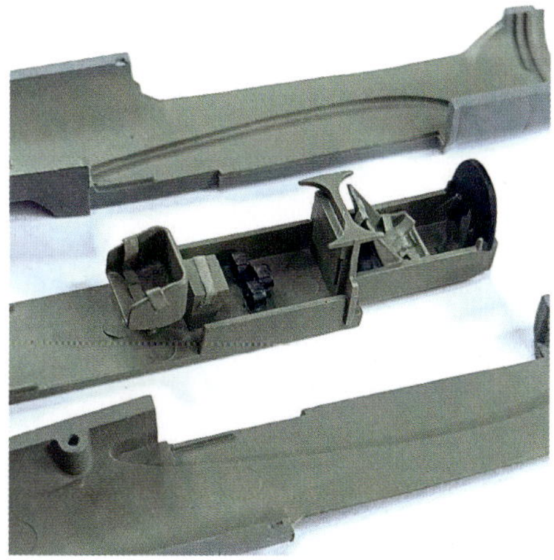

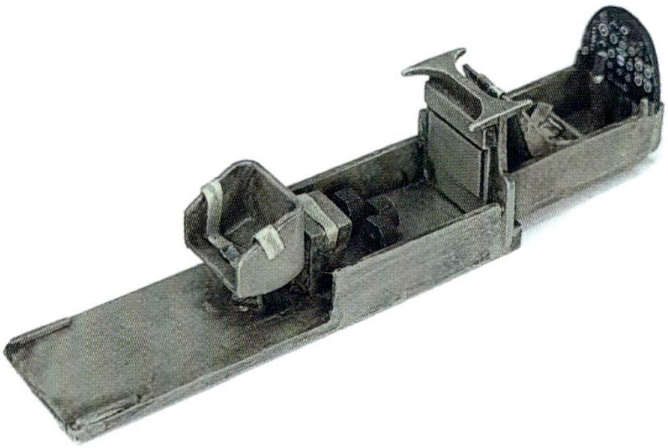

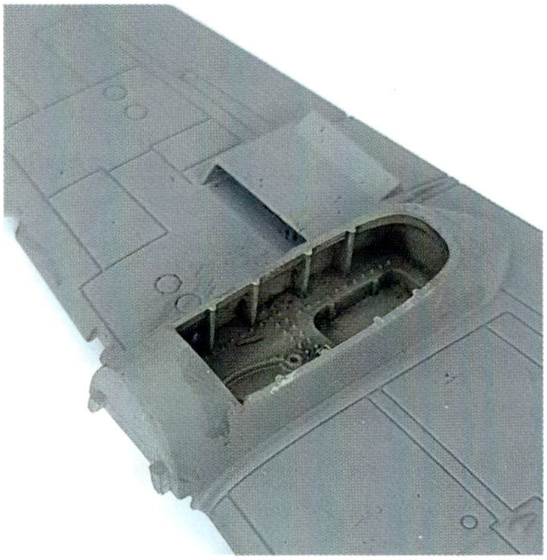

Paint the whole of the interior in RLM 02 *Grau* and then the instrument panel and the magazines for the cannon black. You can dry-brush the magazines and the edges of the pilot's and gunner's seats with gunmetal or aluminium paint to simulate some wear and tear on them.

We can then pick out the seat belts in khaki or paint the crew, depending on the build you are doing. I've given this cockpit a wash of some clay-based weathering product to enhance the detail, although you can either ignore this or use a different product if you prefer.

Area	Brush used	Paint used
Cockpit and wheel well area, undercarriage components and inside of undercarriage doors	Airbrush or size 3 round brush	Humbrol 240 RLM 02 *Grau*
Cannon magazines, instrument panel and grip on control column	Size 2 round	Humbrol 33 Matt Black
Dry-brush chipping on seat and cannon magazines	Flat brush for dry-brushing	Humbrol 56 Aluminium or Humbrol 53 Gunmetal
Seat belts	Size 1 round	Humbrol 26 Khaki
Shadow areas	Size 2 round	Ultimate Weathering Wash Dark Dirt

3) Assembling the aircraft

Assembly of the aircraft is now pretty straightforward; however, there are a few friction points of which you need to be aware. The Bf 110 went through many different iterations throughout its career and most model kits break down into a somewhat modular fashion to allow for the boxings of different versions. If you aren't careful, you can end up using the wrong parts in a build.

This extra degree of complexity also requires a greater degree of dry fitting and parts preparation to ensure that everything fits as it should. Take your time with it and you should be ok.

While most of the airframe is fairly straightforward, you'll also need to add a few small parts to this build, notably the nose machine guns. These can be protected during cleaning up of the seams and general handling of the model by adding some foam or sponge over the parts, and you can tape this in place if necessary.

With the airframe mostly assembled, I'll then set about cleaning up all the join lines and seams.

I prefer to add the canopies prior to painting; however, you can choose to mask off the cockpit opening and fit the canopy later if you prefer. I've masked and added the canopy now to avoid harming the paintwork later on, and also added the rear machine gun. This is a very delicate part so I shall also be keeping it protected with some sponge when I'm not working on the surrounding area.

BRUSH-PAINTED BF 110

This aircraft has had the canopy painted in RLM 02 and then been given a coat of grey primer. You could use black; however, it is far easier to get smooth coverage over grey than it is a black base with brush-painting. The upper surfaces of the aircraft have the fighter camouflage of RLM 02 *Grau* and RLM 71 *Dunkelgrun*, with RLM 65 *Hellblau* painted along the fuselage sides and lower surfaces. The sides of the aircraft are also heavily mottled with the surface colours. If you wish to use an airbrush to replicate this camouflage pattern, the guide for the 1/48 Bf 109 will serve you well.

1) Paint RLM 65 *Hellblau*

As light blue covers so much of the airframe and is also the lightest colour we will be using on the model, we will paint this onto it first. You may need several applications of paint to ensure an opaque finish. Keep the paint thin and use a broad brush and you will get a good result. The broader the brush, the more likely you are to eliminate brush strokes when working on large areas such as this.

Area	Brush used	Paint used
Fuselage sides, tail, lower surfaces, undercarriage doors	Size 4 round	Humbrol 65 Light Blue

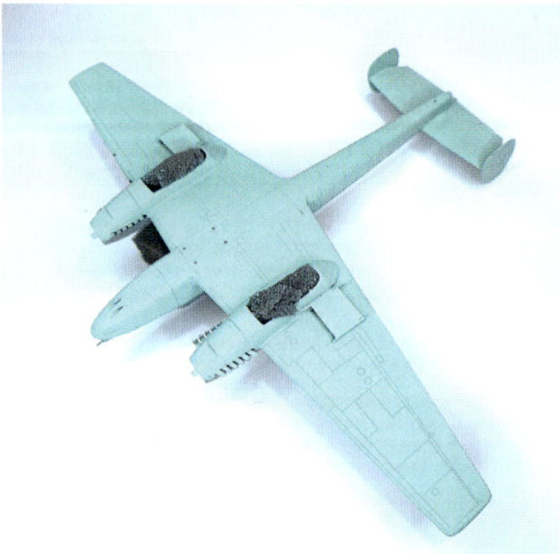

2) Paint RLM 02 *Grau* upper surfaces

We will now paint the RLM 02 *Grau* areas of the upper surface. The aircraft appears to have had a rough, soft demarcation between the upper and lower colours so we can paint the pattern in without masking. Again, as this is a fairly light colour let the tone build up over several thin applications.

Area	Brush used	Paint used
Upper surfaces and top of fuselage	Size 4 round	Humbrol 240 RLM 02 *Grau*

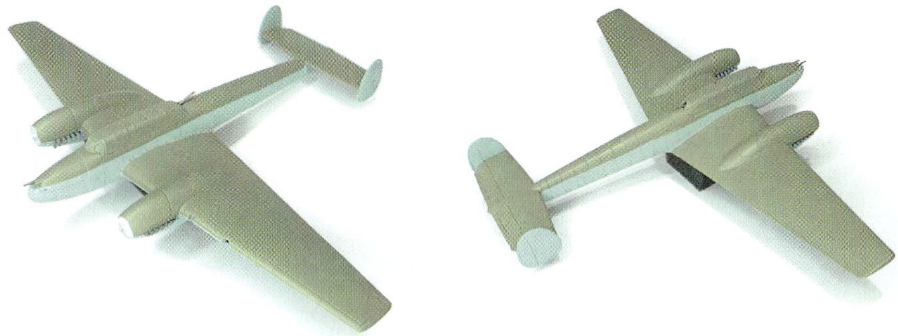

3) Paint RLM 71 *Dunkelgrun* camouflage

Once the RLM 02 *Grau* is dry, we can paint in the camouflage pattern. Again we won't be masking the pattern, although you can if you'd prefer to. The disruptive scheme follows a standard pattern so stick to the

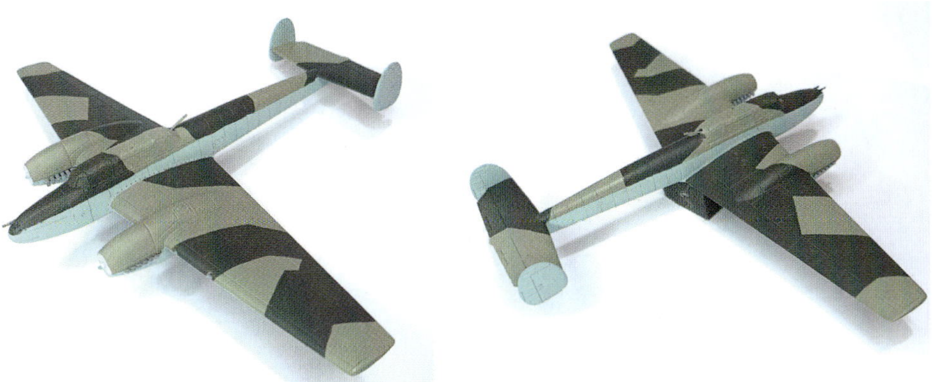

shapes shown in your kit instructions. We will use a smaller brush this time to ensure more precision when applying the camouflage pattern.

Area	Brush used	Paint used
Upper surfaces and top of fuselage	Size 2 round	Humbrol 242 RLM 71 *Dunkelgrun*

4) Grey mottling

To apply the RLM 02 *Grau* mottling on the fuselage and tail surfaces, we will first mask off the top surfaces of the wings. While we want a softer demarcation between the fuselage colours, we want to keep the wings clean. A line of thick masking tape along the wing root will be sufficient.

To apply the mottling, we will use a small piece of sponge to stipple on the paint. Dab some paint onto the sponge, check how much paint is on it by stippling some onto a piece of card and then, using a stippling motion, apply the grey onto the fuselage sides and tail surfaces. You can repeat the stippling motion to build up the opacity of the patterning.

Area	Brush used	Paint used
Sides of fuselage and vertical tail	Sponge	Humbrol 240 RLM 02 *Grau*

5) Dark green mottling

We'll finish off the camouflage by stippling on some dark green. To get a fine mottle, you can cut the sponge into a tighter shape such as a triangle.

This point will give you more control in how you apply the darker parts of the camouflage patterning. This aircraft had a fairly loose patterning of the green so we will just apply the pattern in small squiggles and dots.

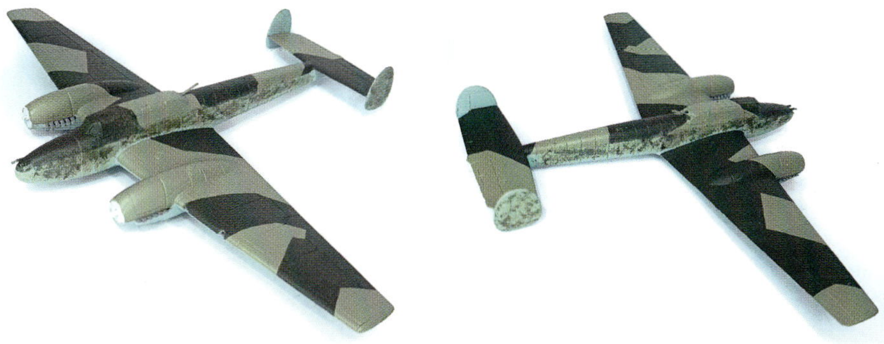

Area	Brush used	Paint used
Sides of fuselage and vertical tail	Sponge	Humbrol 242 RLM 71 *Dunkelgrun*

6) Finishing off

We can now add the transfers, complete the final assembly of the model and add any weathering you may wish. This model has had a clay-based

wash, some chipping and some exhaust staining to give it a weathered appearance. As mentioned earlier, this kit has had aftermarket used. These are identical in their application to the kit markings.

AIRBRUSH METHOD

This time we will be priming the model in black. This will allow us to build up the tones of the camouflage and create a visually interesting and varied surface finish. Instead of working from lightest to darkest colour, this time we will work from darkest to lightest as each colour will then build up in richness of tone. This pattern will also require a significant amount of masking tape to replicate the sharp edge of the camouflage.

Note that you can still brush-paint this pattern and I'd also recommend the masking, although if you are confident you could paint it without. Colours will remain the same for brush-painting.

1) RLM 70 *Schwarzgrun* base

We'll begin the painting proper by spraying on the RLM 70. Mist the colour on to start with to give yourself a base from which to work up. Once that is touch-dry you can begin to fill in individual panels with increasing amounts of opacity. By working on the individual panels you will get some subtle variation in tone across them, even though you are using the same paint with no alterations to the mix.

Leave the model to dry at least overnight. You will be masking and handling the model a lot so you need the base layer of paint to be fully hardened off before working with it further.

Area	Brush used	Paint used
All upper surfaces of the aircraft	Airbrush	Humbrol 241 RLM 70 *Schwarzgrun*

2) RLM 71 *Dunkelgrun* camouflage

We will now spray on the camouflage pattern. Again, lightly mist on the green paint before going back to fill in each individual panel. However, when painting camouflage it's important to keep spraying past the edge of

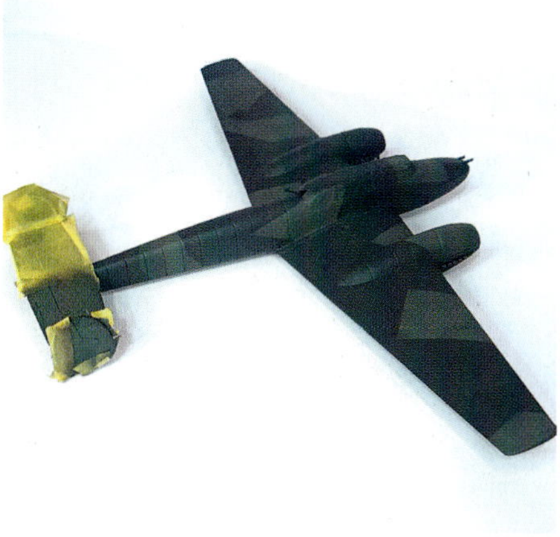

the tape otherwise it may appear as if the pattern is a raised component on the aircraft. Again, leave the model to dry overnight and then mask on the demarcation line between the upper and lower surface colours.

Note that I've left some of the masks on the tail in the images to save remasking them for painting the under-surfaces.

Area	Brush used	Paint used
Camouflage of upper surface	Airbrush	Humbrol 242 RLM 71 *Dunkelgrun*

3) RLM 65 *Hellblau* undersides

With the upper surface painted, we can turn our attention to painting the undersides of the aircraft. Build up the opacity of the blue by misting on several light layers until you are close to the desired final tone before finishing off with painting the individual panels. If you do not have the pale blue colour at its near finished tone, then any subsequent work will create too stark a contrast and the model may end up looking like a patchwork quilt. Don't forget to spray any small parts and the undercarriage doors in the process.

Area	Brush used	Paint used
Lower surfaces, antennae and undercarriage doors	Airbrush	Humbrol 65 Light Blue

4) Finishing off

We can now remove the masking tape. Be careful how you do this, and peel the tape off slowly so as not to pull any paint with it. Once all the tape has been removed you can neaten up any damage or paint bleed and give the model a spray of varnish, with either flat or satin being fine.

Once the varnish has dried thoroughly I'd recommend giving the model a buffing or polish with some very fine wet-and-dry paper to remove any paint ridges that have built up around the masking. With this done, give the model another coat of the varnish.

It is now time to add the transfers, apply any desired weathering and finish painting and assembling any small parts and sub-assemblies that are not currently on the model. We can apply another coat of varnish to unify the finish, and then the Messerschmitt Bf 110 will be complete.

6

Masking

One of the biggest complexities of aircraft modelling is masking. Whether this is for canopies or camouflage patterns it can be daunting to do, and can even run the risk of damaging your paint finish if not done properly. Key areas for masking include canopies and transparent parts, camouflage patterns and open areas you have already painted such as wheel wells.

In this chapter we will look at a few ways to mask canopies and openings, with camouflage being dealt with as it occurs in the painting guides. We will also be discussing some of the products you can use for this purpose.

MASKING PRODUCTS

Before discussing particular techniques, it's probably worth identifying some of the masking products available and their ideal uses.

Masking tape

Broadly speaking, there are two types of masking tape readily available. There is the standard white masking tape that you can buy in most artists' shops. This has a fairly low level of adhesion and tends to be a little inflexible.

These factors tend to have the effect of allowing paint to bleed under the tape, even when painting with care. The white masking tape does have the benefit of being cheaper, however, so is excellent for masking areas that need protecting but do not need a tight join such as within the centre of camouflage patterns. It's also excellent for making seat belts due to it being pretty thick!

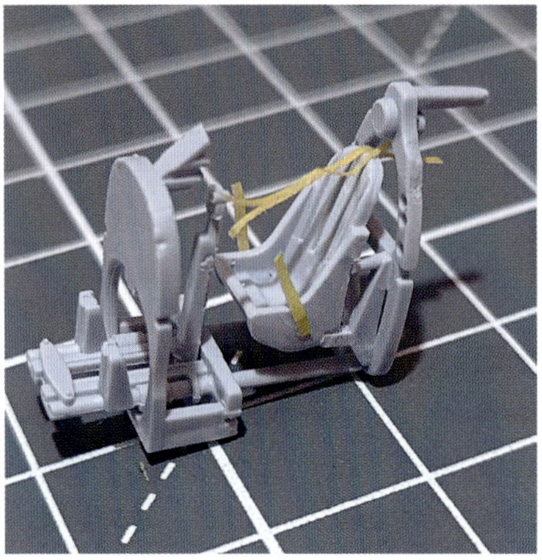

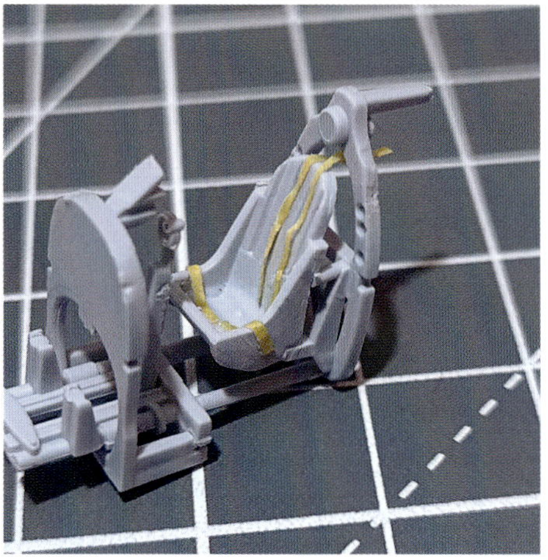

Of more use to modellers is Japanese Kabuki tape. A primary brand is Kamoi, which should be relatively easy to find from online stores. This tape is also sold by the Tamiya Company as Tamiya tape. This product has a high degree of adhesion while being unlikely to harm the underlying paint. The tape is flexible so will conform well to curves and complex shapes. Paint bleed is minimal, although it can still occur.

It is not recommended to use standard adhesive tape or parcel tape as this will leave a glue residue as well as harming the surface of your model.

Another useful benefit of masking tape is that it's great for making the doped lined gun covers fitted to British fighters!

Liquid mask

These products are a liquid rubber or latex-type solution. Humbrol Maskol is a famous exemplar of this type of product; however, Vallejo Liquid Mask is also widely available.

The products are simply painted onto the area you wish to protect, and when they dry they create a rubbery skin that can be easily removed when you are ready. These products are good for masking off areas that are curved or sweeping such as RAF camouflage patterns. However, they do have a few significant weaknesses too.

Firstly you need to be sure the mask is being painted exactly where you want it. Due to their rubbery nature it is very difficult to reshape or alter some of the contours once the model is masked. Liquid mask can also dry clear, although glossy, so it can be quite hard to see.

The masks can be delicate too, and if you knock them it's easy to pull or tear the mask. It's also tricky to get straight lines such as the demarcation between the upper and lower surfaces of an aircraft. This is best left to using masking tape.

This may sound negative, but they are very useful products and it's worth keeping a bottle. They can also be good for tacking small parts into place. One final caution though: liquid mask can quickly ruin a paintbrush so use an old one to apply it.

Masking putty

Putty can be useful for masking models, and some people use Blu or White Tack or plasticine. However, there are also specialized modelling products available to use as such as Panzer Putty or AK Interactive Elastic

Putty. These putties are very useful, especially for airbrushing. They can take some practice, but are quite forgiving in allowing you to lay out the shape of a camouflage pattern and then shape the putty to the surface if you need a hard-edged pattern.

The putty is of less use when brush-painting, and is also very prone to knocking or damage during handling. Still, it can be handy for masking the camouflage on British aircraft.

Thin masking tape

Some 2mm masking tape is a very useful addition to your tool box. It can be used to ensure sharp demarcations on difficult shapes such as the blown canopy of this Spitfire as it conforms to curves much more easily and without distortion.

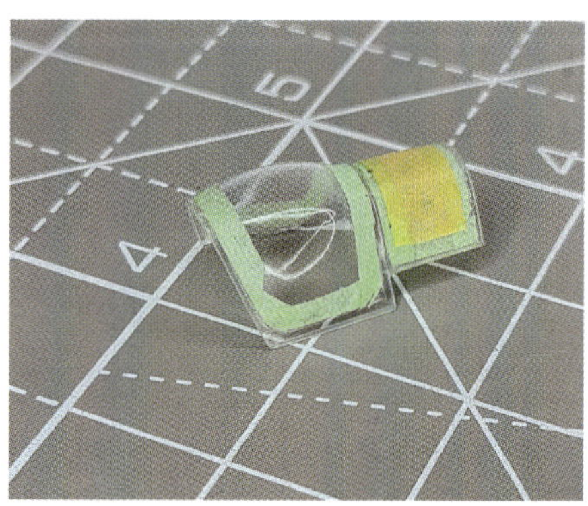

The 2mm tape also has its uses when masking camouflage patterns for the same reason. On this Messerschmitt it is being used to get a tight line along the wing root before applying camouflage mottling.

Canopy masking

Canopies are probably the single biggest hurdle in aircraft modelling. The transparent parts are such an obvious and visible part of the model that any damage or imperfections become so much more noticeable.

The easiest method of masking transparencies is to use a pre-cut masking kit designed for the model. Those are very self-explanatory and come with instructions so aren't necessary to describe in detail here. For more complex aircraft such as bombers with multiple panels in their canopy glazing or aircraft such as the Messerschmitt Bf 110 they can be very much worth the price of purchasing just for the sake of making life easier.

When painting the clear parts, the simplest method would be to trust in your ability to freehand the framing. This can be quite effective, and if you are using acrylic paints any excess paint can be scraped off with a cocktail stick once it has dried.

For a more consistent finish, however, masking tape is recommended. You can either cut thin strips of masking tape to build up the framing or draw the shape of the panel onto tape before cutting it out and adding it to the model.

DRAWING AND CUTTING

For making your own masks for more complex canopies, the most reliable method is to cut your own from some larger sheets of tape. Here's how to make them.

1) Creating a template

This is a rather more complex method, but essentially has you making your own masking kit for the transparencies. Firstly we will place a relatively large piece of tape over the panel we want to mask and then use a cocktail stick to burnish it to the surface. Once the tape is pressed into all the corners of the panel, we will use a mechanical pencil or fine pen to trace the shape of the canopy panel. It can be tempting to cut the masks while the tape is on the canopy; however, avoid this as you will damage the plastic.

2) Cutting the template

We will then remove the tape from the model and place it on a cutting board. We can then use a new, very sharp knife blade to cut out the part. A steel rule can be useful here to ensure you get a straight line to your cut.

3) Fitting the template

We can now add the template to the model, and repeat this process for the rest of the aircraft's transparencies. You will now have a reliable and consistent set of masks to paint your aircraft's canopy. Just make sure that the masks are pressed firmly onto the model in case any adhesive qualities have worn off on the cutting mat.

COCKPIT AND WHEEL WELL MASKING

Wheel wells and cockpits are typically best painted before being added to the model. These areas can also have some delicate parts inside so care must be taken to protect the paint.

Packaging foam is ideal for masking or blocking out these areas and the cockpits of open canopy aircraft. If you do not have any you can use sponge cut to shape, and if necessary you can use a little liquid mask to tack the foam into place.

7

Transfers

Transfers or decals really bring a model to life, and they are the most commonly used way to add national markings, serial codes and insignia. While you can paint these markings on with the use of stencils and masks, for the purposes of this book we will be sticking with decals. These can be a little tricky to apply if you are not used to them, but there are a few tricks to really making them look painted onto the surface of the aircraft.

The vast majority of transfers available are the waterslide variety. These are images printed onto a carrier film and held on a sheet of paper that once dampened loosens the bond with the paper and can be slid from the backing paper onto the model itself.

Two problems occur more than others when applying transfers. The first is the transfer creasing or not conforming to the detail on the model. This is caused by the carrier film of the transfer not being able to settle into and around details, either because the transfers are too thick or the detail is too pronounced from the surface of the model.

The second and perhaps more frustrating issue is silvering. Silvering is when the transfer has small air pockets between the transfer and the surface of the model. Many sources recommend using a gloss surface if you are going to apply transfers, although this is not really necessary. The silvering is caused by a surface not being perfectly smooth under the transfer, creating little pockets of air. In theory, the gloss surface is smooth enough to eliminate this risk; however, a well-applied flat finish will give equal success. You can always give the surface of the model a polish with some very fine (3,000 grit or finer) sanding sticks or wet-and-dry paper to be sure.

There are also additional techniques you can try which we will cover later in this chapter. There are numerous products to treat transfers to help them melt into detail on the model, but a simple way to get transfers to fit around tight curves is to cut small nicks into the carrier film. This should give the transfer a greater ability to settle into the necessary shapes and also remove any trapped air pockets.

For uneven surfaces you will need to ensure that the transfer is properly pressed into the model by rolling a cotton bud over the detail and gently pressing it into the surface once the transfer has had a few minutes to dry in place to reduce the risk of accidentally moving it.

For best results, apply transfers after the basic painting is complete but before you do any weathering.

SIMPLE METHOD TO APPLY TRANSFERS

This is the most basic method of applying transfers, and is also a good foundation to work from with all other methods of applying them.

1) Soak transfer

First trim the transfer from the rest of the backing sheet. It is best to work with one at a time rather than soaking the whole sheet in one go. We will then dip the transfer in a bowl of warm water and then lay it on a sheet of foam. After about thirty seconds the transfer should be starting to move. Slide the transfer onto the model and then position it where you need it.

2) Set into position

Leave the transfer for five to ten minutes and then gently roll a cotton bud over it. Be careful not to move the transfer. You can then repeat rolling the cotton bud over the transfer and applying a little gentler pressure with each pass. This will settle the transfer to the surface of the model.

SETTING SOLUTIONS

There are many setting solutions for transfers on the market. Most consist of a setting solution and a solvent while others are just a single setting solution. However, the two-part products such as Micro Sol/Set and Ultra Decal Fix do tend to be more reliable and give better results. These products work by essentially fixing the transfer to the surface and then melting it slightly, causing it to shrink to the surface of the model. They are the best way to give a painted-on look to transfers.

1) Setting solution

Soak the transfer as previously described and while it is soaking add a little setting solution to the surface to which it will be applied and then apply the transfer. Once you are happy with the position of the transfer, carefully burnish the transfer with a cotton bud and then apply another layer of setting solution. Then leave it for approximately twenty minutes before proceeding to the next stage.

Brush used	Paint used
Size 2 round	Micro Set

2) Fixing solvent

Once the transfer has had some time to settle into position, we can then apply some solvent. Ensure you have done all the burnishing you need to do before you go on to this stage as the transfer will be very delicate until it has fully cured.

Simply paint some of the fixative solvent over the transfer and leave it to dry for a few hours. As this product will be breaking down the transfer to the surface of the model, be careful you do not knock or touch it as this can ruin the transfer. In addition, some fixatives can be fairly strong and have the potential to damage paint. While they are fine to paint onto the model, any sort of contact with them is likely to harm the underlying paint.

I'd also suggest giving the model a coat of matt varnish once the transfers are dried. This should give them a very pleasing painted-on appearance.

Brush used	Paint used
Size 2 round	Micro Sol

When using setting solutions, it is not unusual to see the transfer blister and bubble as shown here. This is perfectly normal and part of the process. Do not be tempted to touch the transfer at this stage as they are very delicate and will settle down onto the surface of the model as they dry.

8

Modelling Flight

Although an aircraft on the ground looks good and it's a great way to show off the interior details or to make diorama displays, to really capture the elegance of these aircraft one must display them in flight. While display stands used to be included in aircraft kits as standard, these have sadly ceased to be a standard component.

While traditionally modelling an aircraft in flight would necessitate drilling holes into the model to insert some sort of suitable stand, the ready availability of cheap, small, rare earth magnets makes creating suitable stands relatively simple and attainable.

While not entirely necessary, to best represent an aircraft in flight you will want to model it with the undercarriage retracted, represent propeller movement in some way and create a stand for the model.

RETRACTED UNDERCARRIAGE

Depending on the particular kit you are working with, this can be as simple as adding a specific part or parts or hugely frustrating. All the kits we've built in this book as flying have had alternative parts for the retracted undercarriage, and these are as simple as using any other parts.

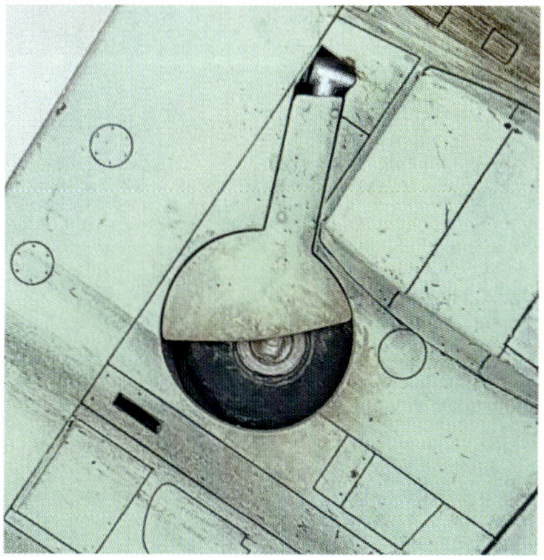

If kit parts are not an option, however, the simplest way to model a retracted undercarriage is to attach the doors to a thin strip of plasticard to the inside face of the undercarriage door. This will serve to brace the parts against the wing, allowing you to fit the doors safely without risking them falling into the aircraft. If the wheels of the aircraft are also visible inside the well, you will probably need to attach these to the undercarriage bay door, and possibly add some of the leg or axle too depending on the aircraft. You will probably need to sand these down a bit to get them to fit properly, but do your test-fitting before sanding or cutting anything.

SPINNING PROP

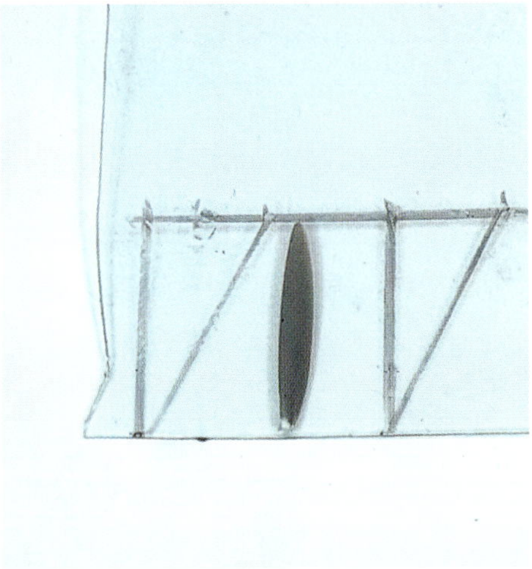

While simply attaching the kit parts for the propeller looks perfectly good and makes a nice display piece, if you wish to create a little more visual interest you can create a spinning propeller effect. My preferred way to do this is to use some thin transparent plasticard. The type used in packaging blister packs is ideal; however, you can also buy sheets of clear plasticard as well.

Measure the length of your prop blade before cutting a fan or pizza slice shape to the same length. For a 1/72 scale aircraft a triangular shape around 1cm wide at its broadest point will suffice, and for 1/48 I'd suggest around 1.5cm to 2cm. For larger scales, increase the size by eye according to what works well.

Once you are happy with the spinning effect, check the fit and size. When this is satisfactory, you can trim off the kit-supplied propeller blades. If you are confident, you can cut a notch into the kit where the prop blade was and this will make adding the blurred effect easier later on.

As these are transparent parts, you will naturally want to avoid adding these until after the model is painted and varnished. It's worth mentioning that this type of plastic does not respond too well to plastic adhesives and bonds far better with superglue. Apply the superglue sparingly to the model, ideally with a cocktail stick or some wire. This will give you far more control over the application of the adhesive.

PAINTING THE PROP BLADES

If you want to really create the effect of a blurred or moving propeller, you can paint on the blade and add some glazed-on effects. This adds a stylized but appealing look to the model. To do so, paint the propeller along one leading edge. Once this has dried, mix some paint and some matt varnish into a very thin consistency before blending this away from the leading edge of the prop. For RAF aircraft, add a yellow line at the tip to represent the warning marking.

Area painted	Brush used	Paint used
Leading edge of propeller	Size 1 round	Humbrol 33 Black for RAF Humbrol 24 *Schwarzgrun* for Luftwaffe

FLYING STAND

Modelling a suitable stand to display your aircraft in flight can be a challenge. Here I will demonstrate how to create a simple stand so that you can then take the idea and expand upon it as you see fit once you are more confident about making them.

For aircraft up to 1/32 scale, the simplest way to make a flying stand is to use some acrylic rod, two rare earth magnets and a suitable base.

1) Creating a stand

The first thing to do is decide how long you want your display stand to be. I'd suggest going no longer than the wingspan of your model and probably a bit less than that. Any longer and the model is liable to be unstable.

My preferred size of acrylic rod for a stand is 5mm, although for larger-scale aircraft or bombers you'll probably want to use 1cm rod instead as this will give you a larger surface area.

To cut the rod you will need a razor saw and ideally a mitre block to ensure a neat straight cut. Once you have selected a suitable length, cut the rod to size. Then, using a two-part epoxy such as Araldite, attach it

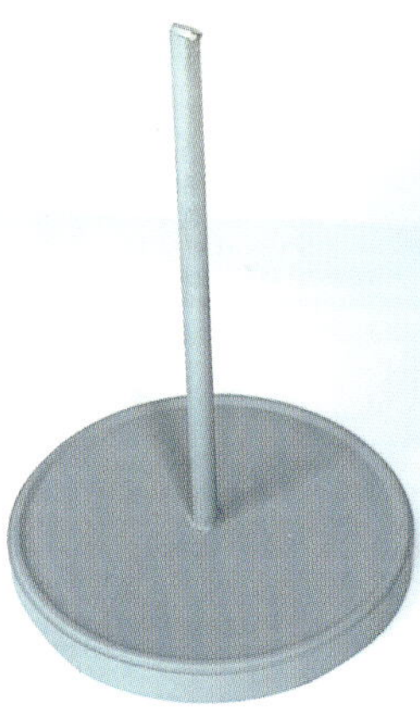

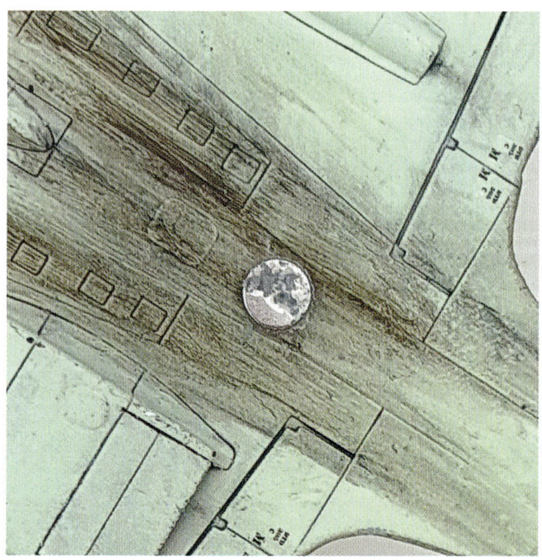

to a suitable base. You can use anything that appeals to you for this at an aesthetic level. Some suggestions are cast resin or plastic display bases, wooden or acrylic bases or any other suitable material.

If you have suitable tools, it's worth drilling a suitable-sized recess into the base to ensure extra strength.

With the stand completed, superglue a rare earth magnet the same diameter as the rod to which the aircraft will attach. Rare earth magnets are thin, flat magnetic discs that are also very strong. Once the magnet is attached, pair it with a second one and mark the back of the magnet that will be attaching to the aircraft with some paint. This will ensure that the polarity is correct when attaching it to the aircraft.

2) Optional step, scenic base

Now, while you could either leave the stand clear or paint it a suitable colour, you can also use this opportunity to create a scenic stand. You can either use the guide for groundwork in the diorama chapter of this book or do something else.

For these particular bases I've used the same acrylic texture paint to create a coastline and then painted the base to represent the distant ground. The water is simply painted with dark blues and then has a few tiny dots and lines painted on in white to represent the waves and breakers before being given a few layers of gloss varnish. The whole base is brush-painted.

3) Attaching the aircraft

Next up is actually attaching the aircraft to the stand. You will need to determine the centre of gravity of the aircraft. Typically this will be around the midpoint of the aircraft, somewhere towards where the rear of the wings meets the fuselage. The easiest way to check this is simply to see where the model balances when you hold it.

Once you have established the centre of gravity, superglue the previously marked rare earth magnet into place, making sure that the marked surface of the magnet is the side attached to the aircraft. Wait for this to dry, and then run some more thin superglue around the edge to ensure that it is firmly held in place.

The aircraft should now sit nicely on the display stand without any need for drilling into the model.

9

Crew and Figures

Figures can give a real sense of size and scale to your models. They add an extra degree of visual interest and are largely obligatory when modelling an aircraft in flight. They also add an extra level of narrative appeal when creating display bases.

Figure-painting is very much a hobby in its own right and has a wholly different skill set to aircraft modelling. This can make painting the crew figures for your aircraft models intimidating. That said, I'll show some replicable techniques here that you can use to paint your figures. I'll paint pilots wearing standard uniforms for both air forces that would be worn by the majority of pilots.

Paintbrushes are worth mentioning here too. As the figures are very small, it may seem sensible to use a tiny paintbrush. However, these brushes have a tiny well or reservoir of paint and will make the flow of paint frustrating. Instead I would suggest a good-quality size 1 or even size 2 brush as long as it has a good fine point. This will give you far more precision and control when working with small details.

RAF FIGURES

RAF pilots wore a variety of clothing throughout the war: leather flying jackets, overalls, tunics and even on occasion civilian jumpers. However, during the period of the Battle of Britain, probably the most common clothing worn by pilots was the greyish-blue service dress uniform along with black flying boots, Mae West life jacket and Type B flying helmet.

Some pilots who had served in the RAF in the pre-war period chose to wear their white or occasionally black overalls or prestige suits as a

(Kent Battle of Britain Museum Collection)

sign of their service; however, the wearing of this was limited to the old hands. Leather flying clothing was also worn, predominantly by bomber crews or those flying at higher altitudes for extended periods of time.

SERVICE DRESS PILOT FIGURE

This figure will be painted wearing the standard flying uniform, and will be ideal for the majority of figures in your Battle of Britain collection. The service dress uniform this figure is wearing was the standard issued to male Royal Air Force personnel and although a different cut, the colours used here can also be used for WAAF figures as well.

1) Basic tones

While we will be adding shading and highlights to this figure, we will start with a process known as blocking in and as the name suggests, this is a case of painting the base tones onto the figure. If you are working in smaller scales or going to be closing up the canopy, this can be sufficient if you do not wish to invest further work into the crew.

As the service dress is the main colour on the figure, we will begin by painting the uniform with RAF blue-grey. You could mix this tone using greys and blues; however, I will be using a ready-mixed dark blue Humbrol paint. Apply the blue-grey all over the figure except the head.

You could choose to limit the blue to just his uniform; however, this is equally effective and ensures a solid tonal base from which to work.

Once the uniform is dry, we can pick out the straps and life jacket in khaki. While popular perception has the life jacket as yellow, this change would not happen until after the Battle of Britain and so the vast majority would have been a khaki colour.

We will pick out the boots in black and the helmet and gloves with dark brown paints. I will cover the painting of skin a little later. With all these areas try to be as neat as you can; however, if any paint does get somewhere you don't want it, you can easily tidy up when the figure is dry.

Area painted	Brush used	Paint used
Uniform	Size 1 round	Humbrol 96 RAF Blue
Life jacket and seat belts, oxygen mask	Size 1 round	Humbrol 72 Khaki Drill
Helmet and gloves	Size 1 round	Humbrol 98 Chocolate Brown
Boots	Size 1 round	Humbrol 33 Black

2) Adding definition

With the basic colours on the figure, we can now start to add some shading to the model. We will be painting darker versions of the previous colours into the recesses of the figure using heavily thinned paint, glazing in shadow. This gives us more control as to how deep the shadows get, and will permit us to have the darkest shadows in the deepest recesses.

Mix some black or dark brown into the previously used colours in a ratio of 50/50 and then thin this to the consistency of a wash. Paint the glaze into the shadows, repeating the application until you have a level of tonal variation with which you are happy.

For the helmet and gloves, we will just thin down pure black paint and apply that to the respective areas to give us a very dark brown final tone.

Area painted	Brush used	Paint used
Uniform	Size 1 round	50% Humbrol 96 RAF Blue 50% Humbrol 33 Black
Life jacket and seat belts, oxygen mask	Size 1 round	50% Humbrol 72 Khaki Drill 50% Humbrol 33 Black
Helmet and gloves	Size 1 round	Humbrol 33 Black

3) Highlighting

We can now finish off the figure with some further highlighting. To do this we will mix ever-increasing lighter tones into the base tone we used. You could use pre-mixed lighter paints; however, I prefer to mix colours as you get more control in the gradients between colours.

For the blue we can mix either a light blue or grey into the base blue. With the khaki and the brown areas, we will mix in a little buff paint. You will be best off mixing in a little of the lighter tone at a time and then painting this mix onto the raised areas of the figure's uniform. You can keep mixing increasing amounts of the lighter tone, painting smaller and neater highlights into the areas of the figure that will naturally catch the lights.

For 1/72 scale figures, I'd suggest only adding one level of subtle highlight to the figure.

Area painted	Brush used	Paint used
Uniform	Size 1 round	Humbrol 96 RAF Blue + Humbrol 90 Sky
Life jacket and seat belts, oxygen mask	Size 1 round	Humbrol 72 Khaki Drill + Humbrol 71 Oak
Helmet and gloves	Size 1 round	Humbrol 98 Chocolate Brown + Humbrol 71 Oak

LUFTWAFFE FIGURES

The standard Luftwaffe uniform was actually very similar to the RAF service dress. It comprised one of two types of tunic, the *Fliegerbluse* or the *Tuchrock*. This was a similar colour albeit a greyer-toned uniform than that worn by the Royal Air Force.

While this would be worn when flying during the Battle of Britain, other clothing was also popular. The standard uniform could be supplemented by a black or dark brown leather jacket which would be a thin, waist-length version.

(Kent Battle of Britain Museum Collection)

Commonly a set of khaki overalls would be worn over the uniform. The *Sommerfliegerkombi* was a lightweight set of cotton overalls used by crews of both fighter and bomber aircraft.

The Luftwaffe generally used black leather flying helmets, boots and gloves, along with light khaki life preservers, although in the Battle of Britain a lightweight flying helmet was also popular.

As the standard uniform was so similar in tones to the RAF one, you can use the same painting guide for the blue parts of the uniform, although I would suggest using light grey as the mixing colour for the highlights. Here we will paint a figure wearing the khaki flying suit.

LUFTWAFFE FLYING SUIT

1) Basic tones

Again we shall begin by blocking in the basic tones of the figure. We will paint all of the figure's clothing with a khaki tone. The life preserver was a very similar tone; however, to create some contrast and visual interest we will paint this a lighter buff colour. Finally we will paint the boots, gloves and flying helmet in black.

Area painted	Brush used	Paint used
Uniform	Size 1 round	Humbrol 72 Khaki Drill
Life jacket and seat belts, oxygen mask	Size 1 round	Humbrol 121 Pale Stone
Helmet, gloves and boots	Size 1 round	Humbrol 33 Black

2) Adding definition

We will now add some shadow to the figure. As the model's clothing and equipment is such a light tone, we will need to use a lighter colour as the shadow. If we were to use black or mix black into the paint, this would alter the tone of the colour and add too much contrast. Instead we will apply a brown wash to the figure. For this model I've thinned some earth paint until it is translucent before painting it over the whole figure. Be careful not to let the wash pool and ensure you do not let the wash flood the detail of the figure.

Area painted	Brush used	Paint used
Whole figure	Size 1 round	Humbrol 29 Dark Earth

3) Highlighting

The figure is now ready to be highlighted. With the wash applied, you may find the colours have shifted to being quite a bit darker. To begin highlighting, and to prevent the colours appearing too pale, we will first paint the initial base colours onto all the raised areas of the figure that would naturally catch the light.

Once this is done, we can mix ever-increasing amounts of white into the base tones to paint further layers of highlighting onto the figure until the desired level of contrast is achieved.

Area painted	Brush used	Paint used
Uniform	Size 1 round	Humbrol 72 Khaki Drill + Humbrol 34 White
Life jacket and seat belts, oxygen mask	Size 1 round	Humbrol 71 Oak + Humbrol 34 White
Helmet, gloves and boots	Size 1 round	Humbrol 33 Black + Humbrol 34 White

SKIN TONES

1) Base tone

Painting skin tones can be as simple or as complex as you like. For this figure, we will use a functional recipe with which you can then experiment once you are confident about using these paints and processes.

We will use some Citadel paints here as they have an excellent range of Caucasian skin tone examples that are readily available.

To begin with we will use a rose tone and paint this over the figure's face. Again, we will use a size 1 brush with a very fine tip.

Area painted	Brush used	Paint used
Skin	Size 1 round	Citadel Cadian Fleshtone

2) Highlight

We will now add a highlight using a light peach colour. The reason for applying this before shading is that it will give a smoother, more organic blend to the tones. Paint these highlights onto the cheeks, forehead, nose, upper lip and chin.

For 1/72 scale figures you could leave the figure at this stage and they would look good once the canopy is in place.

Area painted	Brush used	Paint used
Raised areas	Size 1 round	Citadel Kislev Flesh

3) Shade

We will now apply a glaze of a terracotta colour. This will add definition to the face and also some contrast between the highlighted and shaded areas. It's important that the paint does not flood the detail as fleshy areas need more subtle shifts in tone to look realistic. You can always lift the paint from the surface with a brush before it has dried if you think there is too much.

Finally, and as a completely optional step, we will thin down some black paint and apply that to the eyes. We won't be doing the whites of the eyes as at this scale it can just create a 'fried egg' effect. If you make the eyes too big, then these can be taken care of by cutting back in with your shade colour.

Area painted	Brush used	Paint used
Recessed areas	Size 1 round	Citadel Tuskgor Fur

Thank you to re-enactor Mitch for allowing me to photograph his excellent flying officer impression. This is very much the day-to-day uniform and equipment worn by an RAF fighter pilot during the Battle of Britain.

Above left, above right and right: *This very rare Battle of Britain Mae West was used operationally in the battle and gives an excellent idea of how the vests had yellow high-visibility areas painted over the khaki canvas.* **(Kent Battle of Britain Museum Collection)**

10

Weathering

Weathering is the process of adding wear and tear to your model. Given the high tempo of operations with aircraft going on sorties multiple times a day, their once clean finish would quickly become worn.

Paint around panels, engine cowlings and access points could chip and wear, revealing bare aluminium. Guns and exhausts led to staining with use. Engines leaked oil and dust was thrown up as aircraft took off from grass runways during the height of summer.

There are dozens of weathering products available on the market. I'll demonstrate a few here, but aim to keep it as simple and accessible as possible. Weathering is an entirely optional step and many modellers opt to not add any at all.

I'll be demonstrating seven techniques in this chapter. However, you can pick and choose those you like the look of and use as many or as few as you wish. When weathering, take a moment to consider how the aircraft would wear; for example, how streaks and stains would form after the paint was chipped. I'd also suggest applying panel lining or other effects that were applied to the whole aircraft before working on more isolated weathering as this can make the model a little harder to read.

PANEL LINING

Adding a wash into the panel lines of the model can enhance the detail, but can also serve to make the model look something of a patchwork. Using a complimentary neutral colour can alleviate this. Using a grey rather than a brown or black wash especially can give a more subtle finish. This is particularly important when working on the lighter colours of the aircraft's under-surfaces.

To produce panel lining, you will need to apply a wash consistency paint to the details of the model and allow capillary action to carry the paint into and around the details. This should not require too much cleaning up, but you could use a cotton bud to remove any excess. As such, I'd suggest using a clay- or oil-based wash as these are far easier to clean up than acrylics.

Enamel washes and fast-drying oils are also a good option, although they do require you to be a little quicker in cleaning the surface of the model. You'll have maybe an hour from applying the wash before you run the risk of some staining remaining on the surface.

I've used a large brush that still has a decent point to apply the wash. When using oils they can be hard on a brush so don't use your brand new expensive ones for this.

Here I've thinned down some artist's oil paint with white spirit and then applied it to the model. I've chosen to use a dark grey colour and used this on both the upper and lower surfaces of the aircraft. Once the paint has become touch dry, I've dampened a cotton bud with white spirit and used this to remove the excess oil paint, leaving the wash in the recesses of the model.

It's worth testing your paints first to see if they react to the white spirit. I'd recommend applying a varnish before working with oils, preferably an

acrylic one to prevent any damage to the surface. A gloss varnish will give a cleaner finish than a matt one as there is less surface residue to hold on to the pigment when you are removing the excess wash.

Area	Brush used	Paint used
Panel details	Old size 4 round	Winsor & Newton Payne's Grey

CHIPPING

Chipping the paint where it has been worn away from use tended to be localized to areas of heavy use during the Battle of Britain period. While there are techniques using chipping fluids or hairspray, these give a more heavily worn finish to the surface than is really required here.

We will apply some silver paint to the edges of the engine cowling and gun access panels as well as along the wing root where the pilot and crew would access the aircraft.

(Kent Battle of Britain Museum Collection)

(Kent Battle of Britain Museum Collection)

For more control, we will use a fine brush to paint some small chips roughly along the edges of the ammunition panels and engine cowling. We will also pick out the panel fasteners in aluminium too.

For larger areas of chipping along the wing root we will mask off the fuselage to prevent any paint spilling over and then use a sponge to stipple on the aluminium paint.

Area	Brush used	Paint used
Edges of panels and fasteners	Size 1 round	Humbrol 56 Aluminium
Wing root	Wedge-shaped sponge	Humbrol 56 Aluminium

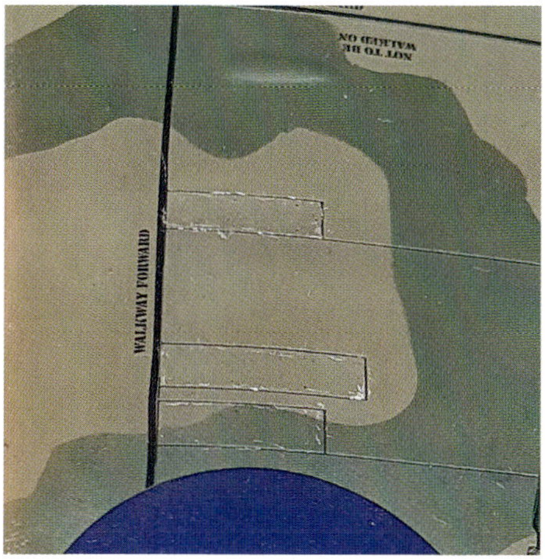

WASH

For a more worn finish to the aircraft, we can instead apply an oil- or clay-based wash over the entire surface of the model. We'll apply the wash over the whole aircraft, ensuring that it is collected into all of the details, and then allow it to become touch dry after an hour or two.

(Kent Battle of Britain Museum Collection)

Area	Brush used	Paint used
Panel details	Old size 4 round	Winsor & Newton Raw Umber or Ultimate Weathering Wash Dark Dirt

REMOVE WASH

We can then remove most of the effect by buffing the surface of the model with a cloth or cotton bud. This may well leave some residue on the surface, especially on models with a matt finish. You can then use a

cotton bud soaked in a suitable thinner to remove more of the residue to add further variation between the panels on the model's surface.

EXHAUST AND CARBON STAINING

When the engines on Second World War aircraft started up, there were considerable quantities of soot and exhaust emissions expelled by the engine and these would stain the surrounding areas of the aircraft.

Similarly when the weapons were fired, especially those recessed into the wings as on RAF aircraft, carbon staining would accumulate leading from the gun aperture. These can be replicated using either paint or weathering powders. Here I will use weathering powders to demonstrate using a different type of product. I've used an old, stiff-bristled brush to paint on a black weathering powder before using the brush to buff it into the desired shape. You could equally well use a cotton bud to achieve the same effect. When weathering black-painted aircraft the exhaust staining

(Kent Battle of Britain Museum Collection)

has a tendency to appear grey so you can use a grey powder to achieve the same effect.

Area	Brush used	Paint used
Exhaust and gun muzzles	Old size 4 round	Humbrol AV0011 Weathering Powder Black

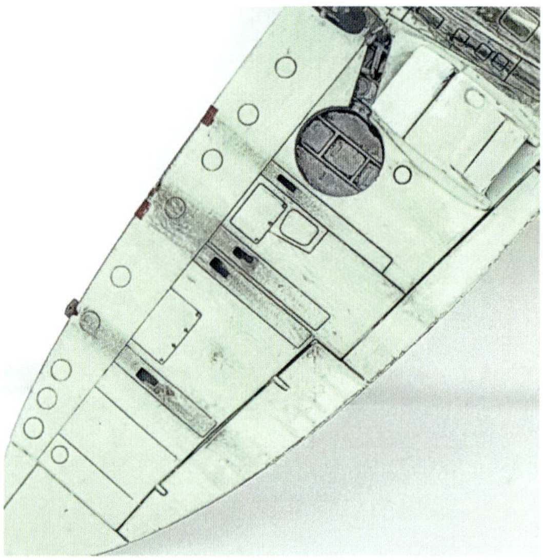

OIL STREAKS

When aircraft are parked on the ground, even the most well-maintained machines have a tendency to leak oil. This seems to be especially prevalent on RAF aircraft, and the undersides of Spitfires especially appear to have ended up absolutely filthy with oil stains.

These stains are easily replicated by painting dots of neat oil paint onto the aircraft where the engine meets the fuselage or wing and then using a flat or chisel brush to drag the paint towards the rear of the aircraft. You can do the same with acrylic paints, although you will have to work more quickly and won't have the option of blending or working the paint as you would with oils. You could alternate this by adding some dark brown oil dots as well to add some visual interest. I have used both paints in the example illustrated.

(Kent Battle of Britain Museum Collection)

Area	Brush used	Paint used
Panel details	Old size 4 round	Winsor & Newton Payne's Grey + Winsor & Newton Raw Umber

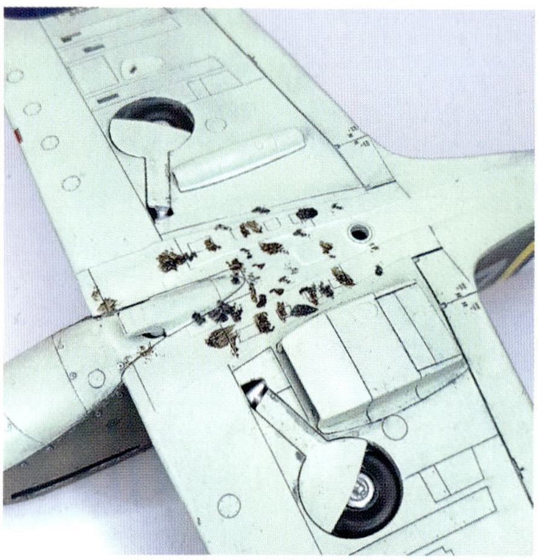

DUST AND DIRT

Aircraft would often be operating from grass runways during the summer of 1940, and as a result would end up getting somewhat dusty or even muddy, especially around their undercarriage and the areas that crews and ground crews would use when working on the aircraft.

To add some dust and dirt to the aircraft we will be using some pre-mixed enamel products designed for the purpose. These are very

(Kent Battle of Britain Museum Collection)

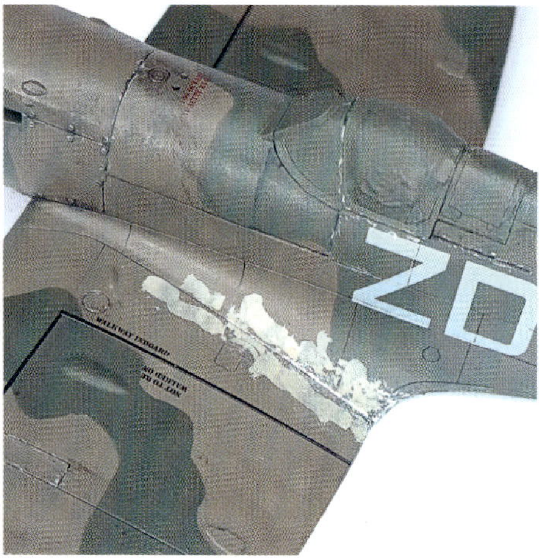

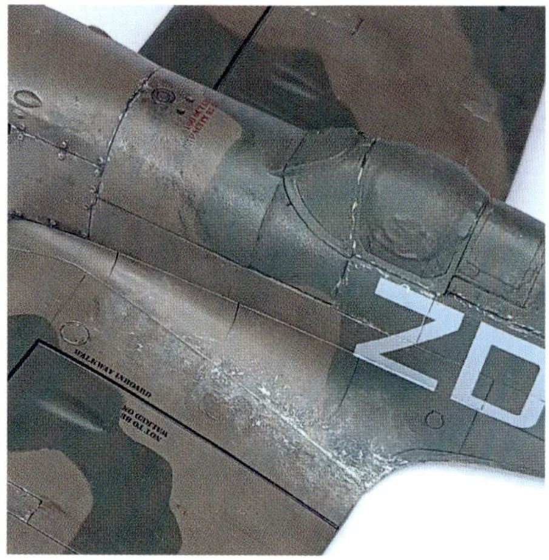

forgiving products to work with due to their long drying times and they allow you to build up the effects by using different earthy tones.

We will apply some dust effects on this model to the wing roots and wing panels where ground crews would be moving on the aircraft. We will also add a little dust to the wheels and wheel well doors. You could use weathering powders or acrylic paints for this; however, I find these enamels are so much more satisfying to work with.

Paint the dust effect into the selected areas and then blend it into the surrounding surface using a suitable thinner. The effect will be subtle, but will represent a light and dusty covering very effectively. You can repeat this process on the tyres and the undercarriage doors as well.

Area	Brush used	Paint used
Walkways and around undercarriage	Old size 4 round	AK Interactive 4062 Light Dust Deposits

11

Display Bases

A nice display base or even a diorama can really set off your finished model into an eye-catching display. While diorama-building is an art in itself and would probably fill a book on its own, I'll describe how to create a simple base for your models. I will also demonstrate how the positioning of models on the base can really affect the narrative elements of the piece.

1) Creating a base

Picture frames make an excellent starting-point for diorama and display bases. They have the double benefits of being sturdy and inexpensive. Wood frames are traditional for bases; however, acrylic or metal ones can look equally as good.

I'd suggest using a dark frame, black or dark brown wood, as these will provide a neat edge without distracting the viewer's eye or pulling attention away from the model. Ideally a frame with Perspex rather than glass is the type to go for; however, either will work. You will also want to remove any fittings or stands at the rear of the picture frame to allow it to sit level when being displayed.

To create a display surface we will measure the inner area of the frame and cut some foam board to size. This is a thin polystyrene-like material backed with card. It is easily cut and shaped, and is ideal for making display bases.

Once the foam board is cut to shape, you may wish to use either some two-part epoxy or a hot glue gun to attach it to the glass or Perspex. To save on masking the frame I would suggest adding the scenic base to the frame after all the painting and modelling work is finished. You may need to add some weight such as a heavy book to the board to get it to dry and settle evenly.

2) Adding texture

Traditionally groundwork has been created using household fillers. These still have their uses; however, for flat bases such as this there are several ranges of textured paints and pastes that cover well and also provide

a good base tone from which to work.

Mask the frame completely, ensuring a good seal between frame and base. You can then apply your texture paint all over. Use an old brush as the textures in the paint will destroy the brush, and apply a flat, even coating. I've decided to add a strip of concrete taxiway to one corner of the base so have smoothed this off with an old business card as the texture paint dried.

Area	Brush used	Paint used
Groundwork	Old size 4 flat	AK Interactive 8018 Dark Earth

3) Painting concrete

If you decide to add a concrete area to the base, paint this in a light warm grey. You could mix this with some mid-toned grey and add some light khaki; however, I'll be using a grey straight from the bottle. I've not done any masking and simply painted this straight onto the concrete area. This may require several coats to ensure a solid coverage.

Area	Brush used	Paint used
Concrete area	Size 4 flat	Humbrol 28 Camouflage Grey

4) Painting earth

We will now add a dusty, earthy wash to the base. Apply this to both the concrete and the soil areas. This is an optional step; however, it will add some realism to the groundwork. Apply a wash of a khaki or earthy tone. I've used an enamel weathering wash, but you could use whichever paint you prefer. While the wash was still wet, I've used an old brush to blend it into the surface and reduce the intensity of the effect.

Area	Brush used	Paint used
Groundwork	Old size 4 flat	AK Interactive 4062 Light Dust

5) Adding grass

Finally, we can add the grass to the base. While you can buy static grass clumps as well as flock, for this we will need loose static grass. I'd suggest lengths of 2mm and 4mm, and two to three different shades. I like to use a lighter green, a darker green and a brown shade, and then mix some of each into a pot for future use. This will give you a realistic mix of tones and lengths representative of cut but not manicured grass.

Apply a layer of thin PVA glue evenly over the areas of soil and then sprinkle on the static grass. Keep sprinkling the grass onto the base until you have a thick, even coverage. Flip the base over and shake off the excess grass onto a sheet of paper. You can tip this back into the pot for future projects. Gently blowing on the remaining grass will prevent any clumping and it will set in a more natural position. Leave the base to dry overnight, and the PVA should dry to a clear, matt finish. If it does not, however, you can spray on some matt varnish from an airbrush or aerosol can if you wish.

POSITIONING MODELS

When positioning models onto a base, adding them at an angle to what will be the main viewing position will increase the narrative and visual dynamism of the model and also allow viewers to take in more angles of the centrepiece at once.

If you are adding figures, position these in a way that enhances the storytelling aspect of the piece with them centred at the focal point. A few different displays with the same models are shown below to illustrate this.

This diorama features a 501 Squadron Hurricane with two pilots discussing their most recent sortie after being greeted by one of their dogs while a WAAF prepares to record the details of their mission.

OVERLOADED BASE

This scene is essentially the same as the finished product; however, some of the empty space has been filled with a truck. It's important to leave some space and allow the eye to engage with the narrative of the piece rather than try to fill every part of the scene.

NARRATIVE ISSUES

This scene has had the Hurricane switched around. While initially quite aesthetically pleasing, the position of the figures and the aircraft doesn't really work as the path the two pilots are taking would have had them colliding with the wing of the aircraft and it also conceals the dog from the viewer.

Pilots would often have access to personal vehicles. These give you a good option of adding an interesting vehicle model to your diorama. (Kent Battle of Britain Museum Collection)

Refuelling vehicles were another common sight around airfields and can give a strong narrative focus to your diorama setting. (Kent Battle of Britain Museum Collection)

Operations blocks such as this were the nerve centre of RAF airfields. Control towers were not particularly present on RAF bases at this stage of the war, so these types of structures are more representative of a typical airfield. **(Kent Battle of Britain Museum Collection)**